WOODBURY

The Twentieth Century Revisited

compiled by

Roger Stokes

Roger Stokes
1st December 1999.

HALSGROVE

First Published by Halsgrove 1999.

British Library Cataloguing in Publication Data

Catalogue Data for this book is available from the British Library

ISBN
1 84114 045 7

HALSGROVE
Halsgrove House
Lower Moor Way
Tiverton, Devon EX16 6SS.
Tel: 01884 243242
Fax: 01884 243325
http://www.halsgrove.com

The vignette on the title page is from a photograph of the interior of St. Swithuns Church taken very early in the Century, and showing oil lamps and chair seating.

Typesetting and layout by Roger Stokes.

Printed and bound in Great Britain by Bookcraft Ltd., Midsomer Norton

Dedication

This book is dedicated to my father the late
Harry George Stokes, (1912-1996).
He was a true countryman who lived through
the most part of this Century and its vast changes.
Sadly he did not live to see this record of the village he loved
but was the provider of much of the information for it.

also

To all those who have gained their livings from the land
in the Parish of Woodbury over past Centuries.

A more genuine bunch would have been difficult to find.

All gone but not forgotten.

Foreword

When asked to write a foreword to this magnificent pictorial record of the past Century in the Woodbury Parish, I felt both humble and privileged. I can think of no more appropriate way in which to celebrate our entry into the Millennium.

Country people say, "You can't have two forenoon's in one day". Difficult to disprove? Yet Roger Stokes, the book's author, comes close. Two years resurrecting old photographs, computer enhancing each one and producing a fascinating record of life in the Parish during the past Century. Consider for a moment two appalling world wars, which removed from our midst so many of those who would have made invaluable contributions to their Parish. We have seen the advent of motor transport, the aeroplane, closely followed by rockets landing man on the Moon and then probing ever deeper into space.

On a more mundane level, I saw the arrival of electricity, banishing for ever those smoking candles, oil lights and stoves. Then the telephone! When I left for the war, farm power was the horse. When I returned it had been replaced by the tractor. Now large implements allow even the largest farms to operate with the minimum of workers.

Yet despite the rush and tumult of present day life, here we have a book which very quietly says, "Wait a moment, and consider those who did much in their times to make our Parish such a wonderful place to live". If you doubt this, climb the Beacon. From there you can see the whole Parish, hills, pastures, rivers, woods and the Common. Stop a moment in the autumn at Ford Water and marvel at the gold of the beech......

Never forget the people, look at their faces, see the strength of character. There were many unforgettable characters in those days. They knew hardship. Nothing was easy. Many had a strict code. A thing was either right or wrong - no halfways!

Roger's father Harry would have delighted in his son's book. He was a man who loved his Parish, gave 42 years service to its Council and 19 years service to the Rural Council. He was instrumental in having a flood prevention scheme put in place after the disastrous floods of 1960. He worked tirelessly for his parishioners. Here was a man who knew how to live with triumph and disaster, and learnt through personal tragedy to treat both those impostors just the same. I am glad that Roger is dedicating this book to Harry Stokes.

Now Roger has followed him in the way which he would have loved. These photographs will last into the Millennium and beyond. I commend it to those of you who value your heritage. Guard it jealously, in memory of those who have gone before. They deserve nothing less.

ERIC WARE.
1921 -

Acknowledgements

The production of this book would not have been possible without the help, enthusiasm and support that I have received in particular from members of the older Woodbury Parish families. These are the people who have the benefit of long memories and family histories and have provided me with in the region of 1200 photographs of life in the Village during the last 100 years.

I would especially like to thank the following for letting me delve into their family albums, or for providing individual information, in alphabetical order by surname:

Dave **Asprey** (Exmouth), Phyllis **Austin**, Mary **Birchmore**, Norman **Bowles**, Raymond **Brown**, Reggie **Brown**, Bill **Chapman**, Don **Clemens,** Jeff **Dagworthy**, John **Daley** (Parkstone), Charles **Dawe**, Valentine **DuBuisson,** David **Elphick**, Sally and Ramsay **Elliott**, Bob **Fox**, Ada **Follett**, John **Glanvill**, Gordon **Hallett**, C.R. **Havill** (Wellington), Nancy **Hollett**, Ed **Kenwood** (New Orleans), Richard **Kinver**, Ken **Lang**, Evelyn **Leach**, Ivor **Loman**, Philip **Middleton**, Gerald and Pauline **Miles**, Bob **Miller**, Margaret and Peter **Myers**, Bill **Pratt**, George **Pridmore** (Exmouth), Hazel **Pyatt,** Brenda **Pyne**, Joan **Sangwin**, Margaret **Sellek**, Gill **Selley**, Brian **Sellick**, Raymond **Shepherd**, Margaret **Smith**, Betty **Spurgeon**, Barbara **Summerell** (Poughill), Heather **Temple** (Chelmsford), Ann **Templer**, Esme **Thomson**, Nigel **Tucker**, Margaret **Vanstone**, Eric **Ware**, Sylvia **Wickenden**, Margaret **Wilson**, Sheila **Wright**.

Also the *Express and Echo* and the *Western Morning News* for access to their photographic archives.

The Author and his father in a field of standing oats
up to his shoulder c.1946.

Contents

Introduction

The Parish of Woodbury is steeped in history, but as I am no historian it is not my intention in this book to go into graphic details from the beginning of time. This detail has been provided already by writers more distinguished than myself; Ursula Brighouse in "A View from the Beacon" and Sally & Ramsay Elliott in their book recording 100 years of the Parish Council.

This book will relate solely to the 20th. Century in the Parish, with a couple of exceptions, and aims to provide a substantial photographic record of life as it happened, both to the people and the fabric of the village scene. It is not my intention to repeat pictures from previous books, but I feel I have to include some for the sake of completeness.

It is quite easy for us to think that we are the only people who have ever lived here, and that things have always been as they are at present. It is of course quite the opposite. One hundred years ago the pony and trap was the main form of transport, the roads were unsurfaced, there was no electricity, mains water supply or sewage disposal system. Most local men were employed in agriculture or associated industries and the ladies developed a living from their homes. Shops of various types were more in evidence even until around forty years ago, but these once essential services have now dwindled to an absolute minimum due to the current ease of travel and communication.

My own family has been resident in the village since prior to 1547, when records began. What changes must have taken place over that period, and what a great pity it was that the camera had not been invented before.

The photographs which form the major content of this book have been generously supplied by the current members of long-standing Parish families. Many are personal family photographs, but they reflect the style and character of bygone days. These families are by general nature those that have been associated with the land, as they are the people who have been in residence more on a permanent basis and therefore been able to retain records of events that took place. They have not in their entirety gone off to find their "fortunes" in foreign lands, and most have a thread of continuity running through many centuries. It is therefore not unusual that they hold the key to the main stockpile of Woodbury history, and I make no apology for the fact that many family names will appear in the book on several occasions, including my own.

Sadly much photographic evidence has been lost over the period, some put on bonfires as families have become extinct and there was no one to pass them on to. Virtually all of the press photographs up to 1942 were destroyed by the bombing of both Exeter and Plymouth during the War, so it is very lucky that the families of the Parish did keep their family albums hidden under the bed, otherwise there would be very little to go on. I have been fortunate to be allowed to research both the *Western Morning News* and the *Express & Echo* newspaper archives, and these two sources have provided a valuable record of the latter half of the Century, particularly in the public domain.

Of the twelve hundred or so photographs that I have scanned and committed to a computer disc for safe keeping, around four hundred of the best appear within these covers. The rest will eventually be catalogued with as much information as possible, and a dossier made available for future historians to be able to research. This will be known as "The Woodbury Photographic Archive". **If there are still any uncharted photographs out there, please bring them to my attention so that they can be added to the overall collection.**

I hope you enjoy taking a look back through a Century of change!

Roger Stokes, Woodbury, Devon EX5 1LL.
1999.

Map of
The Parish of
Woodbury

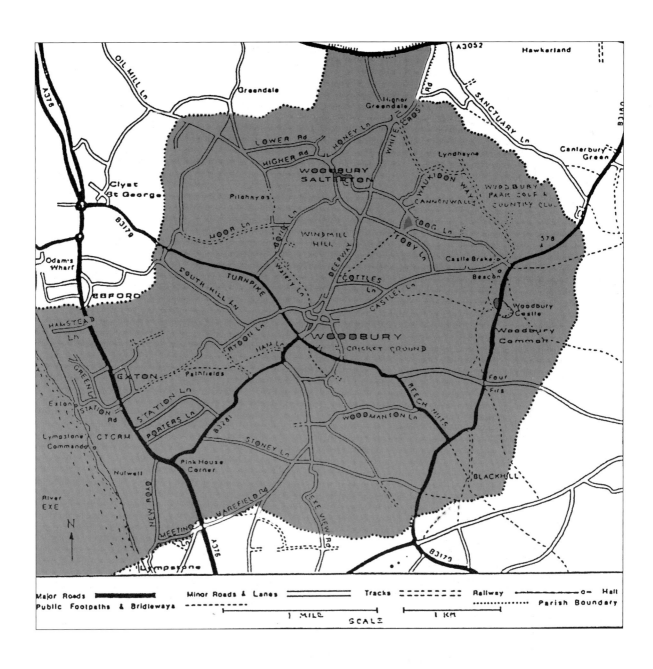

1999

The Early Years

One of the first major events of the 20th. Century was the death of the long reigning Queen Victoria on 22nd. January 1901. This brought with it the inevitable memorial services throughout all towns and villages in the land. The one at St. Swithuns is well documented by the two photographs below. It was obviously a major occasion carried out in a very formal manner. The Woodbury Volunteers were much in evidence, as was the all male choir. The dwarf lady standing in front of the church door was called Jenny Wiles, and she lived in the small cottage in Broadway now called "The Studio". Her brother was a policeman who was reputed to be over six feet tall. Maybe it is him in the lower picture.

The Woodbury Volunteers pictured on Fairfield Lawn following the above service.

Not long after, in 1903, saw the ending of the Boer War. A large crowd of villagers gathered on the Arch for a heroes' welcome home for those that had survived the conflict.

A carnival atmosphere prevailed and the ladies turned out in their bustle skirts with the gentlemen also in their best attire.

The Arch of course had no tarmacadam, but generally differs little to the present day. It was to be the scene of many more similar gatherings throughout the Century.

The sign "The Princess Separator" on William Abbott's shop wall is still there almost 100 years later. This referred to a machine for the separating of cream from milk which Abbott used to sell in his general store.

No doubt these ringers pictured outside the West door of the church in 1905 peeled the bells in celebration. They are seen here before going off on their annual outing. They are from l - r standing: C Stamp, B Stamp, J Morrish, S Marks, G Glanvill, J Down, W Down. Sitting: A Stamp, E Pile (Captain), H Leach, H Hitchcock.

The Street Scene

The Post & Telegraph Office c.1900

The Post and Telegraph Office at this time was situated at the top end of The Arch, and was operated by William Daley who classed himself as a Grocer, Draper and Stationer. He succeeded his father in the business and remained in these premises until he built a bigger and better shop on the site of the present Post Office in 1912.

During his time in this shop and in his capacity as a stationer, he commissioned a series of postcards of the village which were of superb quality and many were hand tinted. Altogether there were well over 100 different cards of the village and surrounds in this early period, which allow us a good view of the village scene at this time.

Looking down from The Arch towards Gillbrook one would have seen Eli Bamsey's shop on the left and the old Cornishes Farm on the right. A good selection of carts, wheels and bits and pieces was always visible. Jubilee Stores is seen on the near left. This was set up in 1897 by Walter Skinner to mark Queen Victoria's Diamond Jubilee.

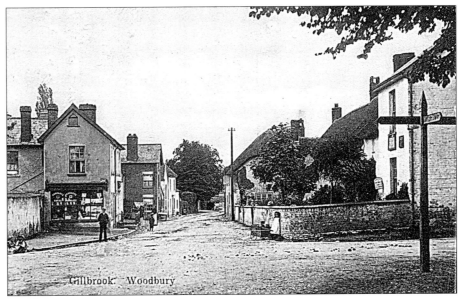

Gillbrook. Woodbury

A little furthur down the road was Gillbrook House, which has changed very little externally during the Century. This was the home of the Ware family, and remains so until the present day. It is now occupied by Esme Thomson and her husband Al. Esme's father was Edgar Ware.

Just across the road from Gilbrook House is the bridge over the Gillbrook, which led to Ham Lane and a beautiful wooded walk beside the stream and across the fields beyond. The scene remains similar, with Brookside Cottage in the background and the small brick built bridge.

Furthur upstream the stream passes through Stile Park, where the children come to innocently play at the waters edge. The card indicates that the field was indeed the allotment field during the 1900-1910 period.

THE EARLY YEARS

Furthur up again you arrive at "Beech Nuts" as it is described on this card. At this point in time it was possible to stop here and have a quiet chat. Not so 100 years later!

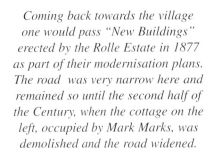

Coming back towards the village one would pass "New Buildings" erected by the Rolle Estate in 1877 as part of their modernisation plans. The road was very narrow here and remained so until the second half of the Century, when the cottage on the left, occupied by Mark Marks, was demolished and the road widened.

Globe Hill is little changed from the scene here in 1904. However, at the top of the hill at this time was The Globe Inn, which was the main meeting place for the village. This was situated on the lower corner of Rydon Lane. It burned to the ground in 1916.

The road from the Castle to Four Firs on the Common is depicted here as a place where you really could get away from it all.

Woodbury Church.
No478.

Up through the main street of the village the view across the Green to St. Swithuns Church was as classic in the early part of the Century as it is today one hundred years later. However, the current large tree can be seen in its infancy here on the right.
I wonder who the small boy was standing in front of the tree!

The other side of the road opposite the Green, Thorns Cottages have changed little over this period, although they are seen here with a thatched roof in 1914.

This 1904 view taken from the top of St. Swithuns tower looking to the East, shows a panorama towards the Common. Preston House is seen dead centre, with, apart from Springhayes, open fields to the Common. An orchard behind Harry Stokes' workshop at Fernlea is where the Village Hall now stands.

Woodbury, Nr. Exeter, Devon

This panoramic scene is from the sister postcard on page 15. How clever it was that the photographer of the time used his talents to provide two pictures which would join up. This half of the card shows Webbers Farm and Haydons Cottage in the foreground and Christ Church on the edge of open countryside in 1904, which was not to be built on until the 1960's.

This shot is particularly interesting as it shows Hunts farmstead (arrowed), long since gone, on the site where the Hayman's bungalow now stands. This is believed to be the only photograph in existance showing Hunts.
The School and Castle Lane are shown, with no Yonderhaye or Longmeadow. Quite a different scene from 1999!

TWENTIETH CENTURY WOODBURY

Towards the northern end of the village the Pound was a prominent feature, and the three pictures here show a "before and after" scene. All the stray animals from the village were impounded within the triangular walls, and released only on payment of a fine.

As time went on, it fell into dereliction and the walls became incapable of holding livestock, so it was eventually demolished and a cross was erected as a memorial to this once much used artefact.

Chown's in the background and Leeches on the right both support superb thatched roofs early in the Century.

In the "after" mode some years later, the view has changed threefold. The memorial cross is quite evident, but also one sees the advent of electricity and telephone poles and wires and a corrugated iron roof on the Leeches, which does not enhance the scene.

Exton and Woodbury Salterton

Unfortunately photographic evidence of the street scene in both Exton and Woodbury Salterton (both wards of Woodbury Parish) is very scant for most of the Century. Maybe this is because neither has been highly populated until the last 25 years, and most of the land surrounding both has been dedicated to agriculture. The postcard below shows the main route through Exton in 1910.

Pupils at Exton School are pictured here.
The school was operational from 1875 - 1947.

The bridge at Exton c.1920.

A general view over Exton c.1920.

The cottages which used to be beside the old Church of St. Andrews.

During the 1920's and 30's sheep used to graze on the foreshore on a grass which was originally planted at Dawlish Warren, but gradually made its way upstream and became a weed.

On a sunny day if you looked towards the land, you might have seen Bill Alford cutting his corn with three shire horses.

THE EARLY YEARS

The pub at Woodbury Salterton is pictured here in 1908. Chickens wander the road before the coming of motor vehicles.

Looking up Village Road from the pub this scene is recorded at the same period of time.

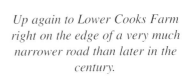

Up again to Lower Cooks Farm right on the edge of a very much narrower road than later in the century.

Again up to Cooks Farm where Mrs Smith is giving the baby an airing in the garden. As everybody is in their Sunday best, perhaps they have just returned from a christening.

In all of these pictures of the 1900-1910 period, thatched roofs predominate.

Early Century People

If you had gone into William Daley's Post Office and store in this early period, you would probably have met some of the following people. Several members of the Berry family were resident at the Green at their agricultural machinery works, J F Glanvill and his wife and son J J Glanvill from Rydon Farm. Perhaps George Wilson from Heathfield Farm or his mother Sarah may have been doing the weekly shopping, or Frank Turner getting provisions for his Devon Yeomanry camp on the common.

JJ Glanvill and his wife, the parents of JF Glanvill, pictured outside Rydon Farm c.1900.

JF Glanvill on his horse in Yeomanry uniform in 1903 pictured outside the family home at Rydon. He was the grandfather of the current JH Glanvill.

Below
The Berry family c.1901
Back row left to right: *Abraham George 1884 - 1934, May 1885 - 1964.* **Front row:** *Reginald 1896 - 1973, Ivy 1894 - 1965, Amelia (Kenwood) Berry 1858 - 1928, Maggie 1897 - 1994, Edwin 1859 - 1916, Ted 1891 - 1960.*

George Wilson 1874 - 1938, pictured with his stallion Jack at Heathfield Farm in 1900.

Abraham George Berry was the first captain of the Woodbury Fire Brigade, and the family was very involved with the Brigade until it was eventually disbanded in 1926. No doubt one of the reasons for this is that their machinery works was adjacent to the fire station, so they were on the spot for quick action. Edwin married Amelia Kenwood also from Woodbury, and from the old established Kenwood cooperage family. Both families had been very prominent throughout the 19th Century, but were to become extinct in Woodbury during the following sixty years.

*Mrs Sarah K Wilson, 1840 - 1920.
She was the widow of George Jacob Bryant Wilson,
and carried the tenancy of Heathfield Farm from
1890 - 1903.*

*Frank Turner of Woodbury Salterton, who came to
work at Heathfield Farm in 1891 at the age of 11. He
is seen here dressed in the uniform of the Devon
Yeomanry before going to camp riding a horse lent to
him by George Wilson in the year 1900.*

*Harry Stokes the first, Bellhanger 1848 - 1915. His
thriving bellhanging and undertaking business was
based at Fernlea, below the present village hall.*

*Bill and Polly Venton from Woodbury Salterton, seen
here on the occasion of their 62nd. wedding
anniversary on 23rd. June 1921.*

Harry Stokes the second, 1878 - 1963, who followed his father into the bellhanging and carpentry business.

Mr Pyne the schoolmaster, who died in 1912.

Mr Fayter the corn merchant and his wife. A formidable looking pair!

Edwin Berry from the Green. A studious looking gentleman!

As the years went by, the economic facts of life became a little grim, and members of some families looked to distant lands to seek their fortunes. The families at that time consisted of many children by today's standards, probably numbering up to eight or so. It was difficult for them all to find meaningful, and profitable, employment in the locality. One such person who took this course was Alfred Stokes, son of William Birch Stokes who died in 1899. He went to Saskatchewan in Canada in 1910 and set up as a farmer, to be followed later by a brother (also called Harry) and two sisters, Ivy and Mary. His sweetheart Elsie Phillips from Ford Farm joined him four years later to get married and have four children. The two pictures immediately below show a very faded Elsie Phillips on horseback outside Ford Farm in 1911 dressed as Dairy Queen for the local carnival, and later as a mother with her husband Alfred in Canada.

meanwhile......

the Ware family was enjoying itself on Budleigh Salterton beach.

Mr and Mrs H Ware with children Eileen and Joy, Mrs Lander (sister), Miss Warner 1st. left, later to become Mrs Edgar Ware, Miss Cleare next left in front row, later to become Mrs Gordon Ware. Picture taken at a family picnic 1904.

and...

the late George Wilson was having his first photo taken on his mother's knee, with his father and sisters in 1917.

The Military

The military was a major part of a young man's life at this point in time. Any young lad who was old enough seemed to join up at the first opportunity. Woodbury Common was the scene for many an annual camp for the Devon Infantry Yeomanry, and also for similar Yeomanries from other counties. Luckily many camps were cataloged in the form of postcards, some of which are represented here. It was altogether a different era from today, where the horse was the main form of motive power and the tent the main form of shelter. There appear to be more horses in the lower picture than probably in half of Devon at the end of the century. The work involved to set up one of these camps must have been an enormous logistical exercise. No just going to the nearest petrol station to keep the motive power going, - loads of hay and feedstuffs would have had to be transported for the horses. By and large the military use for the Common has changed little over the century, due to the parish's continued association with the armed services. However, the means of getting there and back has changed drastically. I wonder what these fellows would think of today's activities.

Sunday service with a wide range of instruments.

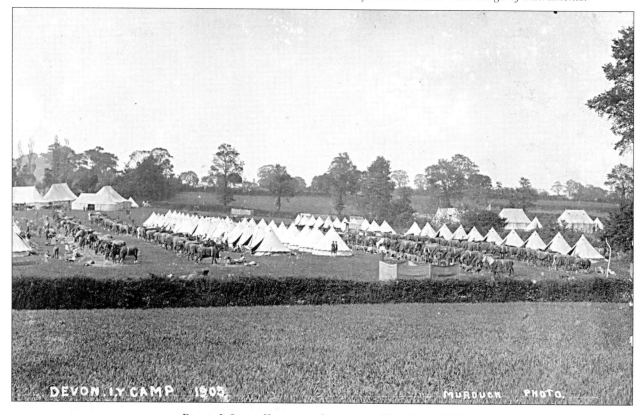

Devon Infantry Yeomanry Camp near Woodbury 1905.

Members of the West Somerset Infantry Yeomanry cleaning their kit at camp on Woodbury Common 1908.

Raising the tent. 1910.

Devon Infantry Yeomanry Camp 1904. The shadow of Woodbury Castle in the background.

These Woodbury men of the Devonshire Regiment were pictured before leaving for India in 1914. This postcard from Bill (Reeves?) to J Glanvill, Rydon Mill, differs from the one in Ursula Brighouse's book as it contains two more persons. However, those present probably include George Crump, George Cook, Walt Chapman, Sam Hawkins, Mark Marks, Edgar Wright, Sid Stamp, Fred Searle, Walt Godfrey & George Carter. Of the other two perhaps one is "Bill".

Similar operations went on through several decades and Eric Ware well remembers in the 20's and 30's being able to hear the sound of up to 100 horses' hooves all the way from Clyst St. George to Woodbury, stopping only for watering at Globe Hill fountain, where they fell silent whilst the horses drank. For the children it was a moment of great excitement.

The motive power of the Military depended on the horse, and quite a number of these animals were supplied by local farms.

The picture on the right was taken at Higher Mallocks Farm c.1914, and had written on the back of it "One for the Army", and shows Bob Havill holding the horse and Will Havill in the background.

The Schools

Woodbury School during the early years of the Century at about the time when Mr Pyne was headmaster. Note the bell turret with spire and the beautiful chimneys.

The picture on the left was taken in 1910 and the one below left in 1920 with the teacher Miss Rickard. It would seem at one time the girls were in the majority. The picture below relates to the 10th. May 1911 when the School was struck by lightning. The bell turret was destroyed and a thunderbolt blew open the school doors, tore across the schoolroom and destroyed the boots of one teacher and one child. The press cutting below gave report of the incident, which left the children "paralysed with fear". The damaged boots are shown here. It's a good job the owners were not in them!

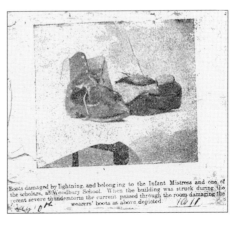

Boots damaged by lightning, and belonging to the Infant Mistress and one of the scholars, at Woodbury School. When the building was struck during the recent severe thunderstorm the current passed through the room damaging the wearers' boots as above depicted.

29

Woodbury Salterton School would have looked something like this at the turn of the Century.

Salterton School Photos
Left: *1908.*

Below: *1910*

Mr Turner who was head-teacher from 1877 - 1920.

So, what else was going on?...

The old Lytch Gate at St. Swithuns, which is seen here with a building on its left hand side, was replaced in 1901 by the Fulford family, and its origins and celebrations are described in the press cutting beside.

The new Lytch Gate is seen here with the building and yew trees gone, and a lamp, which was funded by a grand concert, erected to give light on the way to Church. It is not currently known what the demolished building was used for. However, the Fulford gift lasts for another Century and is still going strong.

"On New Years Eve a very pleasant evening was spent in the Schoolroom, in connection with the presentation of a new Lytch Gate to Woodbury Parish Church, when Mrs Langdon Fulford kindly entertained the choir, ringers and workmen of Messrs. Stokes and Summerfield. The latter had helped in the work of making and erecting the Lytch Gate. A supper and social evening was arranged. The Lytch Gate was recently put up to the memory of Mr C R Fulford, who died in S. Africa. Among those present were Mrs and the Misses Fulford, Sir Chas. Pearson, Rev. and Mrs Godfrey Bird, Messrs. Lear, Hallett, Hy. Stokes senr and junr., and Summerfield. The Vicar was unable to attend. At 7.30, the company, in number 53, sat down to an excellent supper, after which the usual toasts were gone through. In the absence of the Vicar, the toast of "Church and State" was responded to by Mr Lear, who took the opportunity of thanking Mrs Fulford and family for their handsome gift. The Rev. Godfrey Bird proposed "The health of Mrs Fulford and family", which was received and accorded musical honours. The remainder of the evening was spent in harmony with music and song. Those who assisted were Mrs Bird, pianoforte solo; Mr H. Fulford, song; The Misses Stokes and Polgrean, duet; Miss K. and Mr H. Fulford duet; Messrs W. Abbott, H. Stokes junr., H. Hearn and H. Hitchcock, songs. The Rev. Godfrey Bird amused the company with a laughable reading, "Sign writing up to date". Hearty cheers were given to Mrs Fulford and her family for their kindness, after which the singing of "Auld Lang Syne", and "God Save the King" brought a very pleasant evening to a close, all agreeing they had spent a most enjoyable time."

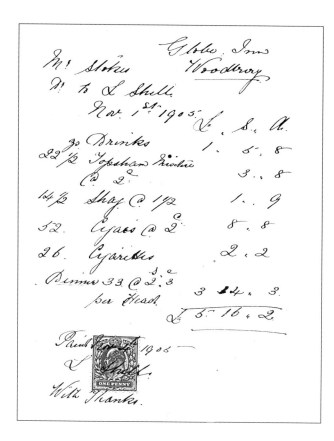

On the 1st. November 1905 Harry Stokes 2nd. married Bessie Pyne from Postlake Farm, and held their wedding party at the Globe Inn which was then situated at the top of Globe Hill and is pictured below. It sadly burnt to the ground in 1916.

The bill for the wedding party is reproduced above, where it can be seen that the 33 guests were well entertained for the princely sum of £5.16s.2d!

These two classic pictures really do reflect this period of time in a rural area. They show the spirit of togetherness in a tight knit village community where it can be seen that it is a case of "Many hands make light work".

The upper picture is a record of threshing time at Cornishes Farm, Gillbrook c.1912, and the lower one is titled "Harvesting at Gillbrook".

Still down Gillbrook way, but in 1925, the annual haymaking was still going on. The jar of cider, the main "fuel" for workers is much in evidence. Those known in the picture are: **Left to right:** *Albie Norton, Trixie Sellick, Albert Gooding, Sam Searle. Emily Davey in front. Edgar Ware far right.*

Again at Gillbrook in the same year are featured Emily Davey, Esme Ware (now Thomson), Nan Ware, Kathleen Searle, Eric Ware and Walter Gooding. The horse and waggon was the main form of transport for all harvest activities up to the 1940's.

As the rabbit was part of the staple diet of all good country people, a day's ferreting was a weekend sport.
Seen here, after such a day is Edgar Ware (right with dog), and A Gooding holding the ferrets.

THE EARLY YEARS

Being a rural area all the country crafts were needed to be known by those living there. These ranged from hedging and ditching, walling and, in particular, any skills which helped in the preservation of food. The "Good Life" system of home production featured very prominently in everyone's family. Little was wasted if at all possible. Classes were organised in all aspects of home economics, and the photo below shows one such cheesemaking class held at the recently aquired Public Hall in 1915.

Cheese-making class at Woodbury 1915.
Back row left to right: Mrs Crook, Mrs H Glanvill, Mrs Ruth Glanvill, Miss Kate Shapland (later Marks), Mrs G Wilson and son George and Mrs H Stokes.
Front Row: Miss Kitty Fulford, Mrs Mason, Miss Bray, Blanche Dagworthy (later Shapland), Alexandra Smith (later Doble), Miss Blanche Fulford.
The small boy with the dog at the front is the author's father Harry George Stokes aged 3, who then lived next door, at Fernlea, the family home and bell hanging business.

A cheese press such as this 100-year-old restored one at Webbers Farm would have been used. It was made by the Berrys of Woodbury.

The inevitable spirit of competition was present as to who had made the best cheese or butter or whatever. A rather humorous, but to the point, comment was observed in the local press, by the judge of a recent butter-making contest.

"The butter making contests, as usual, excited a great deal of interest, and, as already stated, the entries were so large that a division of classes had in some cases to be effected. Generally, the work was well done, and some excellent butter was produced. It was somewhat singular, however, to find in one or two instances that competitors who had previously won prizes were beaten by novices. The explanation of this seemed to be supplied by the circumstance that the latter had had the benefit of recent instruction, whereas the former had apparently neglected to keep themselves in practice, and so lost the advantage of the lessons they had received. To those who are interested, the hint may be seriously taken to heart."

The Stokes' family bellhanging business was, as has been previously stated, based at Fernlea just below the present Village Hall. Their work in the early period consisted mainly of the manufacture of oak frames which were built into the structures of various church towers all over the country, upon which the bells were hung. Whilst predominantly operating within the South West, sometimes their work took them as far as Yorkshire, and it is thought at one time they did some work on York Minster. They built and installed the oak frame for St. Swithuns in 1897, ready to install a new treble and 2nd. to make a complete peal of eight in 1898. Eventually oak made way to cast iron and steel for frames, and they adapted accordingly. The Woodbury oak frame lasted until 1956, when it had to be replaced due to rot where it met the wall. However, by then the bellhanging tradition in the family had been replaced by "Stokes the farmer". The bells themselves were cast and retuned by the famous Whitechapel foundry in London.

If you look at the tarpaulin covering the bell frames in the lower right picture on this page, and look back to the lower picture on page 15, you can see the same tarpaulin in the Fernlea yard with the workshops behind.

Harry Stokes & Son,
Church Bell Hangers,
Woodbury, R.S.O., Devon.

Rings of Bells, to any number, hung on the most approved principles, and Bell Frames made and fixed in Iron or in Oak.

Old Bells Re-cast. New Bells supplied.

The Ellacombe Chime Hammers fixed.
Bell Ropes supplied.

Harry Stokes & Son, having had a considerable number of years' experience in Church Bell Hanging, with confidence solicits the patronage of the Clergy, Churchwardens and Ringers generally.

The Stokes bellhanging team in 1906.
Sitting from left: *Harry Stokes senr. and junr.*
Second left, Emanuel Hawkins; 4th. left, Tolman (foreman); next Jimmy Lark (Blacksmith); Bert Leech in white apron and Sam Coles.

Below: *A cast iron frame ready for delivery at the Fernlea works. The shadowy outline of the popple wall and the house of Webbers Farm can be seen at the back of the picture.*

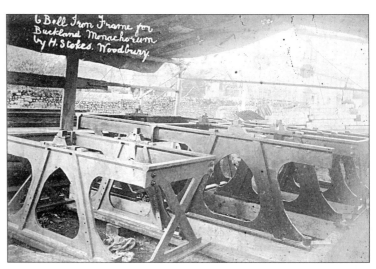

Left:
Harry Stokes 2nd.

The work of bellframes and bellhanging must have been hard graft at this period in time. There were no hydraulic lifts, electric drills or equipment that we have become used to. Everything was lifted by block and tackle and tripods as seen here for the loading and unloading of the wagon transport. Hoisting bells weighing sometimes several tons, had to be negotiated up through a series of trap doors in the towers. One slip or an error could have been rather nasty.

A consignment of bells and a new frame awaiting despatch to St. Michael Caerhayes in Cornwall in 1911.

A variety of work was undertaken at Fernlea, ranging from shoeing horses and burying the dead, to general building and repair work. A typical invoice from the firm would be itemised almost to the last nail, and from some of their accounts one would know exactly how many nails there were in the house. On a more sombre note funerals varied in price depending on how comfortable you wanted to be. Two examples are shown below.

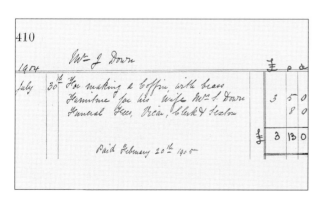

No.001   *15* Shares.

The Woodbury Public Hall Company,
LIMITED.

Incorporated under the Companies (Consolidation) Act, 1908.

CAPITAL - - - £300.
In 300 Shares of £1 each.

This is to Certify that *Mr & Mrs Samuel R Gale*

of

are the holders of *Fifteen* Shares of £1 each, numbered *one* to *fifteen* inclusive, in the above-named Company, subject to the Memorandum and Articles thereof, and that there has been paid in respect of each of such Shares the sum of One Pound.

Given under the Common Seal of the Company this *25th* day of *November*, 19*10*.

The Common Seal of the said Company was hereunto affixed in the presence of

Wm H Fulford

Harry ...... } Directors.

Tom E. Lear Secretary.

The main village meeting place had been the Schoolroom for many years since it was opened in 1871. However, many of the parishoners became dissillusioned by the rules and regulations of booking the rooms and on November 5th. 1909 at the annual bonfire a group of people led by Tom Lear went around the crowd present and obtained pledges of loans totalling £250 towards the prospect of setting up a private company called the Woodbury Public Hall Company. Their aim was to provide a hall free from the Church or the School and operated by the parishoners. The Company set up with a share capital of £300 in £1 shares, as a loan to be repaid later and with an annual dividend. Just over one year later on 25th. November

1910, the first fifteen shares were sold to Mr and Mrs Samuel R Gale, whose certificate is shown above. Most stayed in force until the 1950's, changing ownership as people died and others took up the shares. Topsham's old tin Chapel became redundant, and was bought by the Company, taken down, brought to Woodbury and re-erected. It served the village well until the 1970's when due to the increase in population a wider and more spacious hall was required, with better kitchen and toilet facilities. During the war years of 1914 - 1918 Hall income got a little sparse and the caretaker had to be made redundant, as the minutes of that year record. It also had military uses for income.

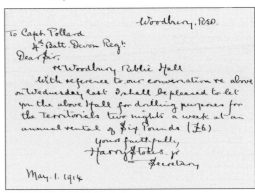

Minute making caretaker redundant.

Letter showing military income.

Woodbury Public Hall Company Limited
Incorporated November 11th 1910

1st Directors Tom E. Lear Broadway
Rev J. L. L. Fulford The Priory
Harry Stokes
Arthur E. Phillips Brook Lea
William C Abbott Lawn Cottage
Harry Stokes Jnr. Broadway House

Meeting of Directors November
Present Tom E. Lear, Rev J. L. L. Fulford
Harry Stokes, Harry Stokes Jnr

Proposed by Tom E. Lear and Seconded by Harry Stokes
that the Revd J. L. L. Fulford be Chairman of
the Directors — Carried unanimously.
Proposed by ~~Harry~~ Revd J. L. L. Fulford & Seconded
by Mr Harry Stokes that Tom E. Lear be
Managing Director Carried unanimously.
Proposed by Tom E. Lear & Seconded by
Revd J. L. L. Fulford that Harry Stokes
with the Managing Director Sign all Cheques.
Carried unanimously.
J H Fulford. Jan 31. 11.

Minutes of the Inaugural Meeting of The Woodbury Public Hall Company.

Transport

Just getting around on foot must have been difficult for these early century people. The roads were probably very muddy as they were not macadam surfaced. The ladies all wore long dresses, and one can well understand why they were mainly black in colour.

Up to 1898 when he died, the Rev. J Loveband Fulford would have been seen daily on his "Reverend Mobile" a three wheeled tricycle which was his form of transport to and from the Parsonage to the Church. When he died the tricycle went into hibernation for a while, but some years later after 1912, Sam Coles was observed riding it past James Hall's Bakery, which used to be the Post and Telegraph Office. It is believed that the trike still exists and after many years stored hanging from the rafters in Berrys Garage, brought out only for "ceremonial duties", it now resides in a museum in North Devon.

Rev. J Loveband Fulford at Parsonage House, Woodbury c.1895.

The pony and trap or horse and cart was the main motive power for the average villager for all of this early period and beyond. The horse obviously had two uses, the second for working the land. These horses were kept in small fields surrounding the village, and brought to harness daily or as required.

Sam Coles on Parson Fulford's tricycle. However, on close inspection of this photograph, this tricycle has handlebars, whereas the one above has brake operated steering. This must have been a major advance in road safety!

The Arch in 1904, with pony and trap.

THE EARLY YEARS

As time went on "public" transport became a fact of life and obviously had a major impact on people's enjoyment for they could now get out and about in groups and see things that had previously been out of reach. Groups as seen here went far afield on outings in the charabancs, but one wonders if it was really that enjoyable, as in most cases the early charas had solid tyres. On one card is written, "If too many people sat behind the rear wheels, the front would come up when going up hills!" Many cards record the fact that these trips went to what then must have been far off places, Bournemouth and Cheddar Caves being two examples. Considering the maximum speed written on the side of the vehicles was "12 mph", I would think that by the time they got there it must have been time to come home again. Goughs Caves at Cheddar seemed to be a very popular place to go, and looking through other books similar to this one, they all have Cheddar pictures.

The top picture shows a Mothers' Union outing c. 1915.

This picture shows a mixed group in their finery about the same time.

41

Salterton liked their share of getting about as well, as this picture shows. **Left to right standing we see:** ?, Robt. Dagworthy, Ike Smith, ?, George Wilson, ?, Ned Auton. **Sitting:** Nance and Fred Hollett, ?, Corny Auton, Win Wilson, ?, Rev. Lewin, Freddie Turner, May and Jane Harris, Amelia Dagworthy, and Mary Wilson.

Date 1930.

This ladies only Salterton group travelled in style on pneumatic tyres and took the pushchair as well! They constituted the Mothers' Union in the early 1920's.

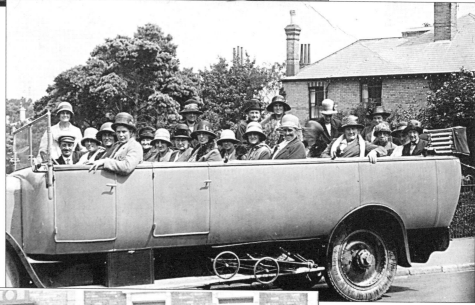

In 1927, Salterton Men's Club went to Bournemouth.

Seen here left to right are: Cornelius Auton, Penberthy (driver), George Wilson, behind him Frank Sellick, Rev. A L Lewin, Joe Auton, Leekie Aird, Horace Auton, John Aird, Richard Dagworthy, George Wilson senr., Leonard Buckland, Samuel Dagworthy, Jack Riggs, Thomas Harris, Sidney Baker, Ned Auton, Frank Welshman, Ernest Smith, Frank Baker.

The Fire Brigade

The Woodbury Fire Brigade in 1900, pictured at Pink House Corner.

The Brigade in Woodbury was formed in the 1860's following a series of devastating fires, both in Woodbury itself and also Salterton. The original fire engine was bought by Robert Brent who paid for it himself, and it was operated by the Woodbury Volunteers. Abraham Berry was the first captain of the brigade, which was horse drawn throughout its entire life. By the turn of the Century William Abbott the ironmonger had taken over the reins, followed later by George Berry. In the 1870's the "Fire Station", seen right in

1914, was built over the brook in Mirey Lane, and everything was housed here.

The brigade continued in force until 1929, when it was disbanded. Fire cover was then provided from Topsham, from where it still comes today. The picture on the left shows the new Topsham machine taking part in the 1935 Jubilee celebrations on the Arch.

43

Inspection of the Fire Brigade accounts for the period 1904-1929 make interesting reading. The cost of each fire is meticulously recorded, down to the last penny, which had to be paid for by the Parish Council. An annual retainer was paid to the Captain of the brigade, and to the team of eleven firemen. Just ten shillings a year in 1906 up to £1.10s. in 1929. The pumpers seemed to have been the best paid, but it is clear from the accounts at the bottom of the page that a decision was made early on in a fire as to whether to try to put it out or not! The fire at the Globe Inn cost very little in pumpers, but that of Parkhayes cost three times as much. Charges were made for hire of horses to pull the engine, somebody as messenger, and someone to supply refreshments. In some accounts, damage to the engine itself was occasioned, therefore causing repair costs.

Woodbury Parish Council.

1906		£	s	d
March 21	Paid Fire Brigade retaining fees			
	Capt Abbott	1		
Fireman	Walter Skinner		10	
"	Hermon Crook		10	
"	William Crook		10	
"	Emanuel Hawkins		10	
"	Walter Chapman		10	
"	William Davey		10	
"	Henry Channon		10	
"	Samuel Marks		10	
"	Henry Sanson		10	
"	Martha Sanson		10	
"	Henry Tellick		10	
	£	6	10	0

WOODBURY.   PARISH COUNCIL.

1929		£	s	d
March 28	Paid Fire Brigade retaining fee + drill			
	Capt Berry	2	5	0
	Fireman E. Burdon	1	10	
	H. Crook	1	10	
	A. Berry	1	10	
	S. Marks	1	10	
	M. Marks	1	10	
	H. Tellick	1	10	
	S. Skinner	1	10	
	J. Tapley	1	10	
	Capt Berry 4 pumpers		4	
	£	14	9	0

The Brigade at *full gallop!*

Woodbury Parish Council

1916		£	s	d
June 13	Payment of Fire Brigade and others for services rendered in extinguishing Fire at the Globe Hotel Woodbury on April 8th 1916			
June 13	Trace & Sons Horse hire	1	10	
	Fire Brigade			
	Capt	1	1	
	Firemen	3	12	
	Pumpers	1	6	6
	Messenger		2	6
June 13	G. Berry Refreshments	1	5	
"	Do repairs to Engine & Hose		2	6
	£	8	19	6

Woodbury Parish Council

1921		£	s	d
January 21	Payment of Fire Brigade and others for services rendered in extinguishing Fire at Parkhayes Farm Woodbury Salterton August 17th 1920			
	Fred Stamp Horse hire	2		
	Fire Brigade			
	Capt Berry	1	14	
	Firemen	3	4	
	Pumpers &c	10	17	6
	Messenger		2	6
	Mrs A Berry Refreshments	2	5	
	George Berry Repairs to Fire Engine &c	1	10	
	£	21	13	0

Fire Committee.

A committee meeting was held on Monday April 30 1928

Present Councillors Daniel. Culford Hallett. Stokes & Tarr.

Councillor Culford in the Chair

It was decided that the Clerk should write the Exeter City Council Exmouth Urban Council & the Topsham Parish Council to ascertain if they would agree to take Woodbury within their area for fire protection & if so upon what term.

In 1928 the future of the Woodbury Fire Brigade was under threat.
The fire committee of the Parish Council entered into negotiations with Exeter, Exmouth and Topsham to see if our brigade could be amalgamated.
Eventually in March 1930 agreement was reached with Topsham, and the Woodbury Fire Brigade formally ceased.
The old engine was put out to tender and attracted two bids. One was £5 and the other was five guineas. Strangely enough, the hose winding gear, bought by Topsham, fetched another £10.
Tenders were invited for the tenancy of the Fire Station, and a long and exciting chapter in the history of our village was finally over.

A Committee meeting was held on Monday March 17 1930

Present Councillors Hallett. Culford, Stokes & Tarr

Tenders for purchase of fire engine were presented. M. Collins. (Blue Ball £5-5-0 M. Davey Exmouth £6.

Councillor Stokes moved that M. Collins tender be accepted, Councillor Tarr seconding it was carried.

An offer of £10 for the hose winding gear + pole was received from the Topsham Parish Council.

The Clerk was instructed to invite tender for the tenancy of the fire station.

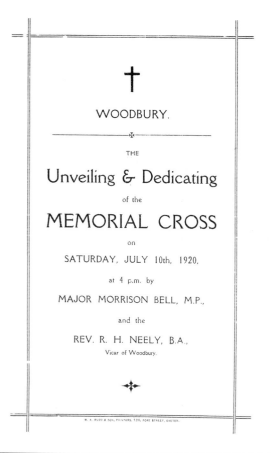

WOODBURY.

THE

Unveiling & Dedicating

of the

MEMORIAL CROSS

on

SATURDAY, JULY 10th, 1920,

at 4 p.m. by

MAJOR MORRISON BELL, M.P.,

and the

REV. R. H. NEELY, B.A.,

Vicar of Woodbury.

Inscription on the Cross:—

**I stand
To the Proud and Glorious
Memory
Of the Men from this Parish
Who gave their Lives in the Great War,
1914–1919.**

Through Sacrifice, to Victory and Life.

Names on the Cross:—

Pte.	Ash, H. J.	Pte.	Henley, W.
,,	Back, F. J.	Stkr.	Lear, S. L.
,,	Back, H. J.	Pte.	Lee, J.
,,	Brockington, F. L. J.	,,	Lock, A. G.
Sgt.	Carder, C. P.	Maj.	Masefield, R.
Pte.	Carter, C. G. B.	Cpl.	Milford, R. J.
Sgt.	Chapman, R. J.	Dvr.	Morrish, A.
Pte.	Davey, A. J.	Pte.	Morrish, T. H.
,,	Davey, J. S.	,,	Pyke, T.
,,	Davey, T.	Gnr.	Reeks, J. J.
,,	Davey, W. H.	Pte.	Sellick, W.
,,	Dymond, H. J.	Tpr.	Shapland, D. J.
L-Cpl.	Eveleigh, F. J.	Pte.	Shell, G.
Pte.	George, E.	,,	Stamp, W.
A. B.	Godfrey, J. B.	,,	Symes, R. W.
Gnr.	Goss, A.	Cpl.	Vickery, J.
Dvr.	Goss, P. G.	Pte.	Welsman, G. K.
Pte.	Harris, C. T.	Dvr.	Wills, T.

The War Memorial was situated on the corner of Broadway and Gillbrook until the 1970's, when it was moved to its current position on the Green, to gain better visibility for motor vehicles entering the main road.

*The builders of the War Memorial in 1920 are seen here. **They are from left to right back row:** H Summerfield, Chas. Summerfield, Harry Lock, Bob Havill, Walter Godfrey, William Crook, Herbert Leach, Harry Sellick, Harry Stokes, Bert Stamp, Walt Veal, A Kilmaster.
Front row: Sam Hawkins, Chas. Morrish, Jim Davey, Walter Chapman, Chas. Norton, Chas. Lang and Reg Summerfield.*

THE EARLY YEARS

As time rolls on into the 1920's Edgar Ware would often be seen riding his horse "Hotstuff". This was a spirited animal which also doubled in the draft of a trap. His daughter Esme (now Esme Thomson) liked to play with her wooden pram and horse. Plus bear of course! The Prince of Wales paid a flying visit in August 1921, and a large crowd surrounded his car as it passed the Post Office. Jubilee Stores was flourishing, and Vera Perry and her sister were regularly seen selling bread, made in her parents' bakery, from a handcart in Broadway.

Jubilee Stores

Esme with father in trap accompanied by Blot the dog!

Esme Ware with her pram in the garden at Gillbrook House.

Vera Perry, later to become Stediford, with her sister Dolly, later to become Dell, a seamstress of high renown, selling their wares.

The Prince of Wales passing through Woodbury on his way to Exeter from Bicton on 17th. May 1921, amid much handclapping and waving.

47

This group of likely looking lads was photographed on the Green one Sunday afternoon prior to going to Mrs B Fulford's Bible Class at 2.30pm. The picture is c.1920, and includes the following people:
Back row left to right: *R Skinner, S Daniels, W Havill.*
Front row: *V Godfrey, A (Bert) Skinner, E Ingleheart, WJ Reeves and HL Jarman.*
(Note the old binder waiting for repair at the Berrys' works.)

This rather faded view of Gillbrook Yard shows Edgar Ware and Sam Searle bringing the sheep home. These once solid brick buildings are of course no longer there. Brookside Cottage can be seen in the background.

If he wasn't in the yard above, the lone figure of Edgar Ware might have been seen walking his cow in for milking.
The picture was taken in Hill Close behind the old Court House.
It shows a fine set of elm trees, sadly lost in the 60's due to Dutch Elm disease, which wiped out all of Woodbury's elms.

The End of an Era

The Wilson family from Woodbury Salterton have been farming there for generations.
They have always been meticulous at keeping records of the past.
Isaac Wilson in the 19th. Century kept the most informative diaries of that period.
The late George M Wilson was no exception to the rule, and some years before his death he spent
the time to record his thoughts and memories of his lifetime in the village. I found that I could not
fail to include these 'reflections' in this book, as they give such a true picture of life which could
be mirrored over the whole Parish at this point in time. Whilst I have interspersed the record with
photographs, no camera could have replaced George Wilson's intriguing facts.

The Village has changed greatly during my lifetime. In the 1920's the cottages were mainly occupied by farm workers and their families. Some were tied to the farms where the occupant worked and had to be vacated when the employment ended. Others were free from any restriction. Many of the cottages were in a bad state of repair because the owners could not afford to maintain them. Probably dating back to the 1600's they were built of cob and roofed with wheat reed thatch which had a life of about 30 years. Sanitation was primitive, usually a bucket privy at the end of the garden path. Main sewerage was still fifty years away. Lighting was by paraffin brass table lamps and candles. Electricity came in the mid 1930's.

At that time the farm worker's wage was £1.10s. (one pound ten shillings) per week and overtime rate 8 - 10 old pence per hour. There were free perks such as milk, firewood, potatoes grown in the field, cider which was much valued, and sometimes a rent and rate free cottage. My late father in law, Mr H Sage of Bridge Farm

the old boy's reaction! Although wages were low, the farm worker never complained and was invariably a cheerful chap quite content with his lot. The work was all manual requiring a lot of strength and stamina which was acquired through starting work at the age of 14. Among the old stalwarts I remember was Frank Turner, who started working for my widowed grandmother at the age of 12. Ned Auton, who once worked for my grandmother, threatened to leave unless she gave him overtime. He was bringing up 8 children on a weekly wage of 12 shillings. Jim Ware, a big powerful man who had the appetite of two men, was sadly accidentally killed on Bridge Farm whilst engaged in felling a large oak tree. Jim Buckland, who daily walked two miles to Stallcombe House, Sanctuary Lane, until his retirement. Sentinel (Saint) Marks who lost a hand through blackthorn poisoning, but continued to work with a ring or crook substituting for his lost hand, doing every job on the farm including driving a pair of horses. He had an enormous capacity for drinking cider. My friend George Carter, who was our neighbour at Cadhayes for 50 years, sadly became a cripple in his prime, but remained cheerful to the end of his life.

Three farm workers taking a rest. All with their bottle of cider. The one on the right is believed to be Lawrence Riggs.

Cadhayes in the 1930's.

engaged a farm worker telling him that he would give him his rent and rates. Some time later the man came to him and said "You are a very mean man, you promised to give me my rent and rates, but I have never received a penny". Perhaps it would be better to draw a veil over

Country folk at that time still spoke the Devonshire dialect, including the children at school. A couple of farm workers' conversations would go something like this, "Mornin' Beel, bootivul mornin' baint it, how be-ee s'morning?" "Aw, not too bad 'Arry, but I wad'n tu wull tother day, 'ad a beet of the snuffles and Missus wanted me ver to go down the quacks ver a bottle o' jol-lop, but I zed hell-a-bout, I bain't gwaine tu do that ver I bain't that papern 'eaded. Twad'n nort anyways ver I wuz zoon better". "Wull Beel, I be glad to yer you be better, but do-ee luke arter yersel". With that they would pass on their way.

The horse still supplied all the power on the farm with the pony and trap providing the speedier transport to Exeter Market on Fridays and for the very occasional outing.

George Wilson's father with his pony and trap and daughter and dog.

Before the coming of the buses my father ran a pony and trap service to Topsham and Woodbury Road stations, also St. Davids and the Queen Street stations. The buses came in the mid 1920's. A firm called Croskells operated a service on the Exeter, Woodbury, Exmouth road while Dagworthy's, later the Sidmouth Touring Co., operated on the Exeter Sidmouth road. After a while, the Devon General Co. took them over.

One of my earliest memories was the fire which completely gutted Parkhayes farmhouse, somewhere around 1919. My father took me to the scene and I remember Woodbury Fire Engine pumping water from the ponds nearby. The pump was manually operated and Perce Sharland told me he helped, but because he was a boy, received no payment. He said, "I cried". I remember the farmer, Jesse Pyle, leaning over the garden wall, bowler hat on the back of his head and crying.

I remember Woodbury Fire Brigade making one of their practice runs through our village. The first we knew was a bell ringing in the distance and getting nearer and my mother would shriek, "Come in out of the way, the fire engine is coming". Then around the bend came the engine with a pair of horses at the gallop, manes streaming. The driver leaning forward, reins firmly grasped in control, the men wearing brass helmets

clinging on either side of the engine like warriors of old pursuing a vanquished enemy. A most impressive and unforgetable sight.

Another memory takes me back to what must have been the summer of 1918. My father had sent my two sisters and me to fetch the cows and we had just reached the gate when a dark cigar shaped object appeared in the sky over Heathfield House. My sisters, who were older than me, panicked shouting, "Germans" and ran leaving me at the gate bawling my head off. Obviously they had heard about German Zeppelins. Many years later I mentioned this to my aunt, who lived at Ford Farm Woodbury and she said, "Yes I remember that well because the mooring ropes dragged over our farm buildings". I can only imagine it was a barrage balloon which had broken free from its moorings.

Salterton School 1927.
Back row: *Joan Meadowcroft, Ron Pyle, Leslie Mitchell, Bill Boyland, Doris Searle, Phylis Searle.*
Middle row: *Girl from Sanctuary Lane, Leonard Mitchell, Ern Pyle, George Wilson, Em Sprague, Roy Sellick, Archie Smith, ?.*
Front row: *Marion Tavender, Dora Sprague, Mildred Mitchell, Isabell Mitchell, George Smith, Peggy Turner.*

I went to school at the age of three, when Mr Turner was approaching the end of his long teaching career and when Mrs Aird would take over. Mr Turner loved music and he would order the bigger boys to take the piano into the playground where the children would sing "Home sweet Home, Keep the Home Fires Burning" and other patriotic songs. Contrary to the present trend, he was a great disciplinarian. I have been told that he would stalk the playground with a pointer behind his back looking for misdemeanours.

There was little entertainment, the piano provided music for a family sing song, it certainly did in our home, for both my sisters could play and people outside my family would call in and give some renderings of old time songs such as "Little Grey Home in the West" and "Charmaine". Wireless began to appear around 1926 -

27 and I can remember my mother taking me to Mr and Mrs Chick's at the Post Office, to hear the Church service from St. Martin in the Fields conducted by the Rev. Dick Sheppard. There were two sets of earphones which we shared in turn. In the winter we would sometimes see magic lantern shows in the Parish Room, which were much enjoyed.

The old Post Office and shop, kept by Mr and Mrs R Chick in the 20's and 30's.

Outside the pub in Woodbury Salterton, when it was run by Walter H Ware c.1912. The small girl is Katie Ware, who was later Jeff Dagworthy's mother.

Old time dances were frequently held in the Parish Room, the music provided by piano. There was a tennis

club and football club, the playing field at Crosshills being kindly loaned by farmer Robert Pyne of Greendale. He was a great sportsman and sometimes held clay pigeon shoots in the same field. There was also a men's club in the Parish Room.

Our village pub was a beer, cider and tobacco house owned by farmer Harry Ware, who also ran a farm. The customers would average four pints per night with about nine or ten at weekends. Few cars ever parked outside in those days.

As children, outings were infrequent. We would be taken once to Exmouth in the summer to play on the sand, ride on the merry-go-round or watch Punch and Judy. On one of the earliest visits I can remember seeing the Lifeboat, still powered by oars, going out on a practice run.

About once a year my mother would take us to visit her father and aunt at Brampford Speke. In the summer, the village children had a great treat provided by the Hon. Mrs Peters at Greendale House. Started by her mother, Lady Dunboyne, it was a memorable day. All would gather at the school and the younger ones would be conveyed in a horse waggon sitting on straw, with the older ones walking behind and holding flags on bamboo poles.

Greendale House.

The lady would be ready to greet us at the gate and everyone had fun on the lawn. Topsham Town Band entertained with rousing music. At the end of the afternoon we all sat down to a sumptuous tea and finally the Hon. Mrs Peters would appear with a large jar containing sweets, which she would distribute to the children. At the end we all gave her three hearty cheers and returned by horse and waggon, singing joyously all the way.

In the 1920's the village road was a peaceful haven for children to play in. The occasional horse and cart or pony and trap would trundle by, but I can remember just four cars which were locally owned. There was Mr

Stubbs of Coombe Park driving his T Model Ford which, in perfect condition, ended its days dumped under a hedge. The Hon. Mrs Peters of Greendale passing in her Armstrong Siddeley. Mr H Hollett of "The Firs" in his large open Wolsely with huge brass acytelane lamps and Dr Darbyshire driving a very noisy open Singer. Occasionally Dr Gaitskill of Lympstone would be seen in a three wheel Morgan or a BSA motor cycle. He had one family as patients.

One car not mentioned was farmer Robert Pyne's. This was his Austin 12 Tourer pictured on Woodbury Common with Win Wilson on board in August 1926. It seems the Common has always been a popular place for boys and girls and cars!

Mentioning Dr Darbyshire reminds me that almost everyone had to pay for his services. In the case of the exceptionally poor, he would waive his charges. People were really ill if he was called upon, for a bill of six guineas was rather daunting. There were no "lead swingers" prior to the introduction of the National Health Service.

Poultry belonging to farmer Harry Ware and Jack Phillips roamed the road all day around the pub area,

much of which was grass covered, pecking in complete peace. The children played hopscotch, whipped tops and truckled hoops. In fact the road was their playing field.

Farmer Henry Sage at Bridge Farm.

As a child, and for nearly fifty years, I saw Mr H Sage driving his pony and trap around the farm. Tom Jennings, a rather dwarf like figure, drove a pony and trap plying his business as a pig and calf dealer. He was illiterate yet successfully made his way through life. If he had made a good deal he would loudly sing some song of his own composition. If the deal had gone against him, he would pass furiously biting his nails. Art Perry and his sister Vera delivered bread and buns and we as boys would run behind shouting "Give us a bun baker". I remember that once, two or three buns were thrown out over the back of the trap.

The Exmouth Industrial Co-operative Society making a delivery to the Pub in 1933. The lady on the right is Annie Ware.

Baker Wheaton also did his round. He was renowned for his dough cake. Baker Hall delivered, riding a trades-man's bicycle. Eli Bamsey drove his specially adapted wagonette, which was a shop on wheels. He sold cotton, wool, pins, needles, boot blacking, polish, laces and kitchen utensils. In fact almost everything to run a home.

THE EARLY YEARS

He sold paraffin, bought rags and rabbit skins. Most of the articles he sold were priced in pennies and the farthing had a strong purchasing value. He would reckon the housewifes purchases like an auctioneer conducting a sale "Three, three half, four three, five half, six pence Madam please". Intentionally or not, it was a little bewildering to the purchaser.

Sam Miller, who had an identical wagonette, came on Saturdays selling similar articles. His horse brasses were always polished to perfection. He would come up our garden path shouting, "Thank you please"! On Fridays an elderly man walking from Exeter would come ringing a brass bell delivering the weekly "Western Times".

Dick Harris delivered the daily newspapers by pony and trap. In the summer he would often return in the afternoon selling mackerel crying, "Hook and line mackl, hook and line mackl .... o - n - l - y a few left"! As a lad he once worked for my grandfather, but was sacked for tarring the water pump handle. He much enjoyed telling me the story.

Road making was a crude operation compared with modern techniques. Tom Pidsley, driving a magnificent former circus engine named "Semper Fidelis" and using a large truck, hauled stone from Blackhill Quarry and unloaded at various laybys in the village area. The local roadman wearing wire mesh glasses, cracked every stone with different size hammers. A stretch of road about 50 - 70 yards long would be selected for repair and the cracked stone was spread evenly using a horse and cart, followed by a layer of sand. Water was sprayed over the surface by a specially built water cart. The steam roller, driven by Harry Sellick, would then thoroughly roll the entire area. Needless to say, the country lanes carried many large potholes. Bill Channon, a local man, was a popular figure among many village boys. He drove a traction engine and threshing machine, visiting the farms in an area which covered many villages. He was still working at 70, spanning a career of 50 years. Fred Curtis, riding a bicycle, delivered the morning mail, and I still remember the aroma of his "Digger Shag" tobacco which hung in the air long after he had passed. Sid Nott walking the afternoon round returned to Woodbury via Sanctuary Lane and Woodbury Common, a distance approximately five miles long.

All the activities which I have described have long passed into history. The horse and nearly all the farm workers have been replaced by the tractor and modern machinery. The cottages are now occupied by commuters to Exeter and the retired. Affluence has transformed the cottages, some of which were rather primitive, into beautiful homes, which their former occupants would never recognise. About four of the original families remain here.

In recent years the village has grown, with new housing, and is still continuing much increasing the population, which has benefitted the school and hopefully the Post Office and Stores.

There is no doubt the newcomers have brought the village alive, which must be beneficial to the community. From a personal point of view I miss the old timers of a long past era. Those farm workers who were the salt of the earth. A type never to be seen again."

George M Wilson.

The late George Wilson's father with Charlie Chick in 1935.

Holy Trinity Church with Spire.

The Wedding of Eliza Dagworthy of Browns Farm to John Stooke of Bridge Farm 1915.
Back row: *Nance Dagworthy, Dick Dagworthy, ?, Hettie Stooke, Bob, ?.*
Middle row: *Rev. Chase, Mr Kenwood, Mrs Sheppard, Harry Dagworthy, Emily King.*
Standing: *Edmund Stooke, John Stooke, Mrs Kenwood, Grandfather Stooke, Grace Stooke, Mrs Wheater.*
Seated: *Mrs Chase, Grandma Dagworthy, Babe Dagworthy, Blanche Dagworthy, Sam Dagworthy, Eliza Dagworthy, Emily Stooke, Grandmother Stooke, Laura Stooke, Miss Wills.*

The Smith family at Cooks Farm c.1910.

The Middle Years

In 1935 the Silver Jubilee of King George V and Queen Mary was celebrated on the 6th of May. There are many photographs of this event, as it happened in the Village, still in circulation. Many, however, were very small, maybe only two inches square and taken with very basic cameras. Some of these have been enlarged to the best of my ability, to feature here. They show the tremendous camaraderie between probably all the social stratas of Woodbury's inhabitants. During these years until around the late 1950's, any major event such as this, was celebrated with a "let your hair down" attitude and great fun was had by all.

Woodbury's own Jubilee King and Queen are seen here depicted by the schoolchildren.
Left to right: *Denis Goss, Joan Davey, Olive Sturman, Doreen Goss (at back), ?, ?, Joyce Sowersby, Betty Ash, Muriel Fox, ?.*

The Military are still much in evidence, being kept an eye on by the local bobby, and followed behind by the public address system.

As they leave the Arch in procession, the motive power is still 1 HP!

The Arch is well decked out with flags and bunting and parishioners stand around chatting socially. No traffic to worry about at this point in time!

The Coach and occupants are well scrutinised by the assembled jovial crowd.

Celebrations also took place at the School, where a grand party was laid on.

The superb original chimneys and bell turret can be seen here.

In total, the Village really had a party! Percy Stediford is seen on the right, about to lead the procession, on Fred Hollett's horse.

At the top end of the Arch, Jimmy Hall's Tea Shop is seen in the background.

The Street Scene Mid Century

Postcards, as always, give us the best record of the changing face of a village. During this middle years period we once again have a plethora of Woodbury cards to choose from. I have included some of the best here. Some are very rare, and I feel that I have been privileged to be able to take a look at them.

During this time the Arch has been much photographed, and its gradual changes can be seen to slowly evolve. Before the advent of large numbers of cars on the roads, the Arch was wide and spacious, but as traffic increased it appears that no-one knew which side of this wide area they should drive on. In the early 1940's an AA patrol-man was stationed here for long periods to "direct the traffic". He is seen here in this first picture, looking extremely lonely, and one could say "What traffic"? However, rumour has it that every time he went off to lunch there was an accident at the cross roads! I think he would have nightmares if he returned today in the 1990's! In the end, in order to make drivers conform to the Highway Code, two islands were installed down through the centre, to keep vehicles apart. It is difficult to visualise that 100 years before this there had been a double row of cottages down through the centre, with another row on the bus shelter side.

*The Arch
in the 1940's
with the
AA patrolman.*

*The Arch
in the 1950's
with dual
carriageway.*

Looking towards the crossroads from Broadway, the square looking cottage on the end of the Gillbrook Cottages can be clearly seen. This was demolished when the other cottages were refurbished in the 60's, to give better visibility for traffic entering the main road. It complemented the removal of the War Memorial from the other corner.
Canada Cottages on the right, are shown in earlier pictures to be complete with balcony, but here are seen with only the floor left. A current photo would show this now gone as well.

Looking down towards the Arch from the Green, the old cottage below Greenleigh can be seen on the right, with the Maltsters Arms on the left. Traffic is very sparse at this point in the century, with clear access all the way.

The top picture shows Haydons, the old thatched cottage which used to be attached to the Church Room. To the left is the old Govetts, which was condemned for human habitation in the late 50's, and replaced by the current estate. Now of course it would have been refurbished!

Behind its roadside exterior the Govetts complex had an internal courtyard complete with pump, with access to five dwellings.

Bill and Gladys Fulls lived here for many years, and both David and Henry their children, lived here in their early years. It was also the home of Dan Box and his wife.

The old lady on the left is Mrs Stevens, and the three girls are Joyce, Edna and Muriel Fox, sisters of the well known Bob Fox. Joyce is now Joyce Biddulph. All have spent time here.

THE MIDDLE YEARS

There is a street scene beyond the Village area, not always seen by everyone and in Sanctuary Lane in 1923, a lady called Mrs Mary Marley who had recently returned from living in Canada, bought a plot of land and built a bungalow. From this she started serving Devonshire cream teas for 1/6d. a time. It became known as "The Tea Bungalow" and stayed in operation for 62 years until it closed in 1985 on the retirement of the daughter of the original owner, Mrs Constance Dupain. Mrs Dupain recalls that people would walk from Exmouth every weekend, or they would come by bicycle or pony and trap. More recently customers would come from afar: from Plymouth, Yeovil and Taunton for their Sunday afternoon treat. During the War years it is recorded that Royal Marines and Polish airmen would visit for a tasty tuck in. The latter would dip their wings in salute when they flew their fighters over the bungalow on their return to Exeter Airport.

The Tea Bungalow in Sanctuary Lane, with immaculate colourful garden, laid for cream teas.

The Tea Cottage, Woodbury Castle.

As people lived a more sedate lifestyle during the 40's and 50's, there was obviously quite a need on such a beauty spot as the Common, to have more that one place for Sunday Tea. The cottage in the Castle provided this for many years and there was a similar establishment at Pine Ridge.

TWENTIETH CENTURY WOODBURY

Improvements were also undertaken to improve the lot of villages with the advent of motor transport.
The press cutting below gives the details of the opening of the Ebford By-Pass, a road which I am sure that most
people, including myself, assumed had always been there!
The gradient of the road as quoted in the following text appeared quite critical at the time to the motor car. Today's
car of course would not even notice it!
The postcard is dated 1937.

EBFORD BY-PASS.

Mr P.F. Rowsell Names Road After Himself.

That since 1914 £65,721 have been spent in widening and reconstructing the main road between Exeter and Exmouth was one of the striking statements made by Mr P.F.Rowsell, of Exmouth, when opening the new by-pass road which commences at the north side of the junction with Odhams Lane, and takes practically a straight course to rejoin the main road at Mount Ebford. The new road is about 480 yards long and had a carriageway of 30ft., with verges of 7ft. 6ins on either side, one of which has been made into a paved footpath. The upper part of the road is in a cutting and the lower part formed on an embankment, enabling a maximum gradient of one in eight on the old road to be reduced to one of one in 14. In spite of rough weather a large crowd gathered for the opening, those present including Mr. and Mrs. P.F. Rowsell, Col. S. Stallard (Chief Engineer to the Ministry of Transport, South Western Division), Messrs. W.E. Poulton (Chairman of the County Council Bridges and Main Roads Committee), Andrew Warren (County Surveyor), J.S. Skillman (Deputy County Surveyor), A.W. Grace (Assistant County Surveyor), Wallace Bardens (Chairman of Exmouth Urban Council), S.Hutton (Surveyor), E.T.

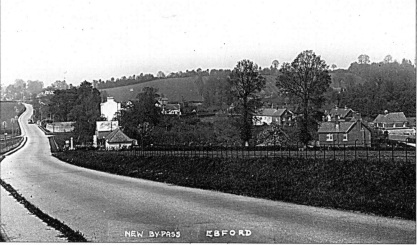

NEW BY-PASS   EBFORD

Linscott (Chairman of Lympstone Parish Council), the Revd. Dr. J.L. Fulford (Chairman of Woodbury Parish Council), Mr. A. Stevens (clerk of Works), and R. Potter (Area Secretary, Automobile Association).

Mr. Coulton, asking Mr. Rowsell to cut the ribbon and declare the road open, said he was going to ask the opener to name the road "The Rowsell By-Pass" because he was certain that it would never have been constructed had it not been for Mr. Rowsell.

Mr. Rowsell said that he was quite sure the new road would be of great value to the public travelling between Exeter and Exmouth. He apologised for the absence of Sir Henry Lopes, who was laid up with jaundice, of Sir Ian Amory, whom they had left at the County Council meeting, and of Major G.S.S. Strode (Chairman of the County Roads Reconstruction Committee), who was indisposed. In a tribute to Col. Stallard, Mr. Rowsell said he hardly knew how this part of

the country would get along without him. He was always helpful, and when a suggestion was made, if there was anything in it, it was always taken up. He was not like some Government officials who said a thing could not be done, and they were not going to do it. A great deal of money had been spent on the main road from Exeter to Exmouth. Since 1914 no less than £63,721 had been spent on it, this sum including the work carried out in the Exmouth Urban district, the Ebford By-Pass, and the estimated cost of the works in hand at Nutwell, Gulliford and Lympstone. They had often been told that the County Council was an extravagent body, but although they estimated the cost of the by-pass at £11,597, the actual cost had only been £10,950. Towards this a grant of 75 per cent was obtained from the Ministry of Transport on condition that they employed 50 per cent of labour from distressed areas. This had been done, and he had not heard a single word against the men brought into the district in this way. The job was commenced in November of last year, and now that it had been completed he was sure it would be appreciated by the citizens of Exeter and Exmouth, and the visitors who came from all parts of the country. The by-pass was absolutely necessary. The Ebford hill had three nasty turnings in it which they had agreed ought to be widened somehow. But they could not see how, and the only alternative was to construct a new road. Mr. Rowsell added that he hoped motorists would appreciate the change in gradient of the hill, and while agreeing that there never was a time when drivers should be so careful as today, expressed the hope that they would not suffer under the new Act. In conclusion Mr . Rowsell thanked the County Surveyor, Col. Stallard, Mr. Skillman, Mr. Stevens and Mr. Grace for their work in connection with the road. He named the road the Rowsell By-Pass and declared it open to the public for evermore.

Mr. Rowsell was thanked on the motion of Mr. Coulton. Subsequently the company took tea at the Rougemont Hotel, Exeter, at the invitation of Mr. and Mrs. Rowsell. Those present included Mr. Brian S. Miller (Clerk to the County Council) and Mr. C.T. Chevalier (Clerk to the Bridges and Main Roads Committee).

Woodbury Road Station, as it was then called, became a busy place during the 30's and 40's.
Locals would walk to Woodbury Road to catch the train to Exeter, and tradesmen would dispatch their produce from
here, having delivered it with pony and trap. Now of course it is called Exton Station.

Back around Woodbury Village, Church Stile had
this facade, as viewed from the Churchyard.

The view farther up the lane towards the junction
of Oakhayes Lane, was a peaceful walking route.
A lot of changes have taken place here!

Woodbury Mills

Woodbury Mills which was situated at Gillbrook served the area's farming community for 65 years in the production and supply of agricultural feedstuffs.
Operated by the Ware family, and more recently by Eric Ware until he retired, it is a unique part of Woodbury's history which has gone for ever.
Eric however, has vivid memories of this thriving business, and I use his story to supplement the following pictures.

On the 24th. June 1915, the Grist Mill, known as the Tannery Mill, was rented to my father Gordon, by his mother Catherine for £39 per year. The youngest of six brothers, he was the only one without a job. Harold Ware had the Tannery, Edgar Ware had the farm and the others lived away. What could they do with their youngest? The solution was to rent him the old stone mill which had been used to grind very large acorns imported from India. When ground up and introduced into the tanpits, they gave that lovely bronze colour to the leather. So he was to use this mill to grind farmers corn. Harold his brother lent him £900 as capital to get started. The only other Mill was a water mill at Rydon, with a very poor supply.

Originally the Mill was driven by an old steam engine. This provided the motive power for the whole tannery. It was replaced by a Fielding and Platt Gas plant, which was fuelled by anthracite.

The Fielding and Platt Gas Plant which powered the machinery during the early years, with valve shown arrowed.

In effect it was a miniature gas works and it relied on a good supply of water. This came from higher up the Gillbrook and was fed down to the Mill from Stile Park, where there was a small concrete dam which led the water into a well. From there it led down into a horse trough thence across the large orchard to the Baptismal Pond, on to the stables and finally into two large circulating tanks before going through a large scrubber, which purified the gas. Just imagine the havoc which floods or frost could cause to such an extended system.

I joined father in the Mills in 1937 aged 15 years and 11 months. Starting at 6.30am. my job was to light up the Gas generator and then add two buckets of anthracite. Then, shutting the generator top, start turning the handle of a very powerful fan. This drove gas through the scrubbers to the engine cylinder. A valve on a pipe shown at the right hand end of the engine was then opened. If the emission of gas burnt when lit, all hands, four of us, would pull and push the two flywheels. If all was well the old thing would start with a resounding "CHUFF"! When working well it would run all day on three buckets of anthracite. When not!, the pulling and pushing of those large and heavy flywheels was an experience never to be forgotten!

In 1937, the National economy was in the deepest recession. Money was short, and farmers would pay what they could, then when they threshed their corn harvest, the account would be cleared. Then the whole process would start again. Early in 1939, when war became inevitable, everything suddenly changed and agriculture became a priority.

In the early days delivery was done by horse and wagon. From Monday to Friday two horses operated with a large wagon, and on Saturday morning two wagons were used to enable the week's orders to be cleared up.

Tom Radford was the carter, with Sid Davey the miller. Sid manned a single wagon on Saturdays, and was never exactly pleased! Grain was largely imported through Avonmouth, and was brought down to the Mill by road by large steam engines and trailers.

The Fielding and Platt, and later a Ruston Bucyrus diesel engine, powered a major network of shafts and pulleys which in turn gave life to all the individual components in the building.
Though probably a current day health and safety officer's nightmare, there was never an accident caused during the Mill's operating life by anyone getting tangled in the belts.

Most Barley came from the Russian Black Sea Ports and was of a very high quality. Just think! - since Stalin slaughtered all those Black Sea peasants, Russia has never again been self sufficient in homegrown grain.

Some barley came from the Persian Gulf, having been threshed by driving bullocks over the sheaves, and it was so full of dust that when tipping it from the sacks into the large bin, you couldn't see three feet in front of you! Maize came from the Danubian Bessarabian basin, known as DBK, the "K" standing for the port of Konstanza. Round maize of high quality came from the Argentine, and was called after the main river, i.e "Plate". Wheat was nearly always home grown, and fed mainly to poultry. Some was sold on for flour to Mallets Mills at Exwick, or Coombes at Thorverton. The picture beside of the main store shows 4 bushel sacks, which for wheat held 2.25 cwts. per bag, barley 2 cwts. and oats 1.5 cwt.

The main store at the Mills held many tons of grain and feedstuffs on the top floor of an old and rambling timber building, which creaked at the seams. All was brought up by chain hoist and manhandled many times.

Two terrible pests were present in the Mills. The first was rats. You were only clear of them when they caught mange! Then they would clear out for five to six months. After the War, the St. Thomas RDC rat catcher kept them down completely. The second pest was fleas. These came in the Persian barley. You caught them in bed at night using a glass of water and a large cake of Lifebuoy soap. Fortunately they cannot swim! There was also Keatings powder.

In 1939 we purchased our first lorry, a 30 cwt. Bedford, and the horses went. Our driver was Mr Reg Marks. In September on Sunday morning Mr Chamberlain declared war on Germany. Two hours earlier the phone rang from Wyvern Barracks in Exeter. A Major announced that he would be arriving at 10am. to requisition our lorry. By 11am. it had gone! Father who always kept calm under pressure, rang up Sam Dagworthy who worked in Exeter at Reid and Lees. Had they got any second hand lorries? "Yes" was the answer, they had a 5 tonner. The deal was done and it arrived on Monday morning at 9.45am., and stayed with us for eight years!

I was called up in February 1941, not to rejoin the business until 1946. The whole of that time was spent in the Far East. I returned to find all animal feed rationed, and farmers were issued with coupons which could be exchanged for feed. This rationing lasted until 1950.

During the War years, farmers had been forced to plough up large acreages and made to grow grain. This almost halted the import of grain, as homegrown wheat generally replaced maize.

Great changes took place when rationing was lifted. The gas plant was replaced with a single flywheel Ruston diesel engine. A 1 ton mixer was installed enabling us to make our own brands of both pig and poultry meals, and coarse cattle foods. It also freed Reg Marks from his daily slog of mixing all feeds by hand. Two lorries were now in operation, a 6 tonner for local deliveries and a 10 tonner which ran daily from Avonmouth delivering direct to farms. A large bulk grain bin was installed, as bulk feed was now taking the place of sacks. Finally a high capacity hammer mill was fitted to do most of the grinding, although we never stopped using the stone mill which was used almost entirely for the grinding of wheat.

In 1954 we changed the Mill's name to Ware & Sons, Woodbury Mills, then in March 1963 we became Woodbury Mills Ltd. My father died in 1968, and on 8th. September I sold to a Unilever subsidiary, Gerald Glanvill. At this point a long tradition came to an end and the Mill finally ceased production.

Eric Ware

Reg Marks seen here mixing the components of a cattle feed by hand, before the days of the 1 ton mixer. The beam scales seen in the foreground were used to weigh the ingredients and the final product. 4 bushel sacks are seen in the background.

Berry's Garage

Berry's Garage in the 1940's with Sam Coles on the left, and Ted Berry on the right.

The agricultural machinery works and garage on the Green, from where Phoenix Motors now operates, could have been classed as the industrial centre of the village. If you wanted anything mended you went there. If the pump in your house which drew the water from the well wouldn't suck any more, or if your bicycle sustained a puncture or broken chain, you went there to get it repaired. During the advance in agricultural mechanisation in this period, there was much expertise to be learned by the Berry family. However, they were the sort of people who would be able to make anything from simple ironwork to repairs in the intricacies of the knotter of the new fangled binder. They were, despite the plain appearance of the building, the skilled craftsmen of their time. They also manufactured cheese presses for the making of cheese and water wheels for the grinding mills. One of their old water wheels now stands as a monument in Exmouth, opposite the Tourist Information Office. This was taken from Withycombe Village Mill when it was demolished. A Berry cheese press is still in the possession of the Stokes family, from which the author well remembers

helping his mother make cheese during the period following the last War. The inside of the garage was dark and dismal, but it was an Aladdins Cave of bits and pieces, with the forge, anvil and a major array of hand tools adorning the walls.

The Berry Water Wheel on display at Exmouth, with Reg Berry and his mother seated.

Ted Berry and Sam Coles (in the cap), seen outside the Garage by the hand operated pumps which dispensed paraffin and petrol.

The Hallett family car is seen outside waiting for a service.

The outside of the building still retains its basic elevations in 1999, although the pumps are long gone.

The darkness seen here in the doorway, echoed right through the place, and as a young boy I nipped in and out smartish!

The bill to the father of Norman Bowles in 1927 shows that a large percentage of all repairs done were to the bicycle. This was of course still the main form of local transport, and I remember my father saying that he used to cycle to school every day to Exmouth. Obviously others did the same, hence all the punctures!

Below is the headstock of a cheese press into which the Berrys had their name cast.

At that time this was current practice for all vendors of presses.

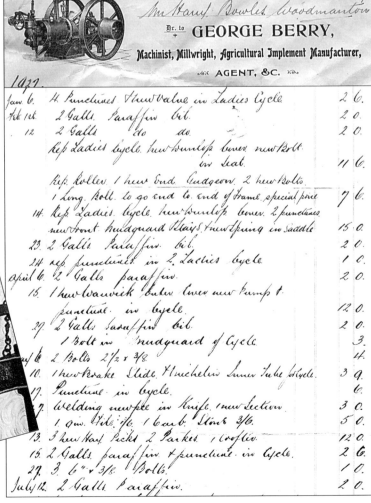

Green, WOODBURY, Devon.

Xmas. 192?

Mr Harry Bowles Woodmanton

Dr. to

GEORGE BERRY,

Machinist, Millwright, Agricultural Implement Manufacturer,

AGENT, &C.

1927.

Jan 6.	4 Punctures & new valve in Ladies Cycle	2 6.
Feb 1st	2 Galls Paraffin Oil.	2 0.
12	2 Galls do do	2 0.
	Rep Ladies bicycle. new Dunlop Cover. new Bolt in Seat.	11 6.
	Rep Roller 1 new End Gudgeon. 2 new Bolts 1 Long Bolt to go end to end of frame special price	7 6.
14	Rep Ladies bicycle. new Dunlop Cover. 2 punctures new front mudguard Stays & new spring in saddle	15 0.
23	2 Galls Paraffin Oil.	2 0.
24	Rep punctures in 2 Ladies bicycle.	1 0.
April 6.	2 Galls paraffin.	2 0.
15.	1 new Warwick outer cover new pump & puncture in bicycle.	12 0.
29	2 Galls paraffin Oil.	2 0.
	1 Bolt in mudguard of Cycle	3.
	2 Bolts 2½ x 3/8	4.
10.	1 new Brake Slide & Michelin Inner Tube for cycle.	3 9.
17.	Puncture in bicycle.	6.
	Welding new pce in Knife. new Section	3 0.
	1 gro File 1/6 1 Carb Stone 3/6	5 0.
13.	3 new Hay Picks 2 Parkes 1 Croftes	12 0.
15.	2 Galls paraffin & puncture in Cycle.	2 6.
27	3 6" x 3/8 Bolts	1 0.
July 12.	2 Galls Paraffin.	2 0.

Other Local Businesses

During this period Woodbury was blessed with many local shops and businesses.
All of the ones following were advertisers in the Flower Show and Gymkhana
catalogues of the 1930's and 40's.
Sadly, local businesses can now almost be counted on one hand.

Clubs and Societies
The Carnivals

Prior to and following the last War, there was always quite a social aspect to the Village. This culminated in the restarting of the Woodbury Carnivals, after the War had finished. After such a long period of hard graft, and with many of the men being away at war for a considerable time, people just wanted to have some fun. There exists a formidable array of old carnival pictures, and some of these appear here. Each carnival would have a "Mayor" and a "Queen". Both were required to sell a maximum number of tickets to attain the post. In particular the contest for Mayor was extremely hard fought, and "dirty tricks" were not unknown, although all in good fun! There was always a Carnival football match at which Perce Sharland had the hereditary position of "Doctor", and revived the flagging teams with his vast array of coloured water carried in his doctor's bag. In those days the fun was good honest fun, and a good time was had by all. The annual carnival procession would line up from a starting point at the top of Oakhayes Lane, and stretch back to the old Webbers Farm to Jack Nash's butchers shop. Here they would be judged before the procession around the village took place. There was a Carnival Season each Autumn, and many of the tableaux would visit neighbouring villages, and I myself remember going to Exminster and East Budleigh in a flying machine which skimmed the trees as it went along. In those days no one seemed to take any notice of danger!

Two or three marching bands would be in attendance, and many solo artistes would be in fancy dress, all collecting money for a good cause as they went along. A carnival fair was always set up on the Green for the week, and I well remember going up on a "Big Wheel" on the Green. Those were the days!

The carnivals went on until the late 50's, when things seemed to change. Television, which had been introduced in the early 1950's took a greater hold on people's spare time, and a general lack of new organising blood took its toll, so in the end the carnivals faded out. However, the memories survive!

Farmer Norman Bowles was the Jester, and used to keep the children entertained in 1949.
Mrs Price, the wife of Dr Price, the village GP, is seen at the back left. She used to present the prizes.
Marion and Pam Jones are spotted just in front of Mrs Price. Now of course they are Pollard and Stuart.

The Crowning of the Queen

The crowning of the Queen was a serious business, and took place in the Village Hall.

Here, WB Hallett is seen crowning Betty Vickery in 1950.

Her attendants are, on the left Joyce Ingleheart and on the right Pat Glanvill, now Bowles.

Here Mrs Price is seen crowning Bonnie Pinch.
All Queens were elected to their much sought after position by who sold the most penny votes.

The picture above depicts the typical type of gathering which took place during and following the crowning.

Many village stalwarts can be seen amongst the large crowd.

Patsy Marks is seen here as Queen, on her "Queenmobile", ready for the off at the head of the Carnival procession. Others in the picture are from left to right: Susan Williams, Pauline Page, Gerald Brown, Barry Drew, Joan Hitchcock and Sylvia Watson.

The Election of Mayor

The election of Mayor was an equally hard fought contest in the general spirit of things.
Each candidate would have an agent to promote his wacky cause. Public meetings were held and promises made,
which can be seen from the following press cutting.

"Mayor" chosen at Woodbury

As a finale to Woodbury's carnival week, the choosing of "Mayor" took place before a large crowd. There were three contestants - Messrs. A J Rowsell, A. Middleton and L.Brown.

Mr Rowsell promised a host of things for the village, and his proposal to stop all income tax at Woodbury met with a tumultuous roar from the crowd. Mr. N Bowles, supporting, argued that Brown had been Mayor before, and what had he done for the village! Middleton too was just a gentleman farmer, and precious little he could do!

Mr. Middleton promised nothing, but his non-stop vocabulary kept his listeners in fits of laughter. When Farmer Brown appeared, a heckler asked where the swimming pool was that he promised when elected "Mayor". Brown retorted: "You haven't been down to my place to see it!"

The upshot was that Mr Middleton was elected "Mayor" by selling 2496 penny votes, and he was adorned with the chains of office, and Mayoral robes by the Carnival Queen (Miss M. Waldron). Mr Rowsell sold 1671 votes and Mr Brown 622.

There have been several "Mayors" over the years, and a few of them are pictured here, either in office or trying to attain it.

Above: Percy Stediford in his Mayoral transport. No expense spared! Below: Touting a vote from Bert Stamp in his pony and trap.

Maudie Yeo with the economy model!

Norman Bowles on the campaign trail with his agent Neil Widgery the Headmaster of the School!

The Carnival Procession

During these years no-one was very flush with money, and the carnival tableaux had to be built on a shoestring budget, with whatever one could get hold of. Nearly all the exhibits were based on an agricultural trailer, which had to be made available several weeks before the event. This was not always convenient if there was a late harvest, as the trailers would be required for hauling the sheaves of corn. Some of the more commercial entries would be lorry based, and so could be more elaborate.

In those days there were no rules and regulations regarding health and safety, and there were remarkably few accidents. Farmers had to get special dispensation from their insurance companies, and the Police generally turned a blind eye as to if you had any brakes or not! Each village organisation would spend many weeks creating their exhibits in an atmosphere of maximum security, not wishing to give their competitors an edge! The following pictures depict some of the end products.

*"One man went to mow"
with Alan Middleton left,
Cyril Rowsell centre and
Victor Fox.*

*"The Armoured Rickshaw"
with, from left to right: Sid Marks,
Bill Chapman and Bill Francis.*

*"Riders of the Range"
with Joan Sellick on pony, Raymond Sellick and Brian Sellick.*

1957
"I had a little nut tree"
Left to right:
Raymond Brown
Helen Middleton
and Philip Middleton.

Below:
The Ford family tableau,
with Margaret Ford, seated
centre (now Vanstone), and
her mother Kitty standing.
Granny Hitchcock in the
background.

left above: *Tim Sellek with his*
"Cottles Comet", apparently
Woodbury's reply to Russia!

below:
The Carnival Ball.
left to right: *Vera Stediford, Percy*
Stediford, Lily Down, Kathleen
Stokes and Bill Boyland.

above:
The "Doctor" attends the Queen Betty Vickery.
Also in the picture are from left to right:
H. Davey, Bill Francis, B. Ledmond, Norman
Bowles, Bill Boyland and Ron Mash.

THE MIDDLE YEARS

The Woodbury and District Young Farmers Club has been a prominent group in Woodbury since 1937, when it was inaugurated following a Public meeting on Tuesday 23rd. of March of that year.

The club covers the parishes of Woodbury, Aylesbeare, Farringdon, Clyst St. George, Clyst St. Mary, Sowton, Topsham, Lympstone, Littleham and Withycombe. Twenty members joined at that Public meeting, and the first AGM took place in the Public Hall on Thursday 8th. April, followed by monthly meetings.

Dr Fulford was the first President, who held the post for eight years, to be followed by Mr GC Daw who was in office for twenty one years. Harry Stokes was the first Club leader, Mr WJ Grabham the first Chairman, Miss MG Tavender from Woodbury Salterton the first Secretary and Mr Gordon Hallett the first Treasurer.

When the club was formed farming was just awakening from a very stagnant period, a period in which little had changed on the land. Compared to today, the cow herds were quite small and the milking was done by hand. Horses were the main motive power. There were just three tractors in the parish, and they were on iron wheels.

By the time the Club was formed young farmers were seeking knowledge and improved methods to meet the great demands that were to be made on the industry.

Thanks to the Club the challenge was met and the food grown to save our country from starvation. Now of course things have gone the other way and there is vast overproduction.

The Young Farmers curriculum revolved around training in practical and social skills, which included stock rearing, stock judging, poultry trussing and judging, rope and gate making, public speaking, drama and generally becoming good citizens. The knowledge of these basic skills have stood many a Woodbury farmer in good stead over the years, and a considerable number have risen to high office within the Parish and also on a wider front.

Following the first meeting twenty seven calves were distributed to members. The first calf show was held at East Budleigh Market on 28th. April 1938. Livestock judging was very popular in the pre-war years, and two members were selected to represent Devon at the London Dairy Show 1938. During the War years several members served in His Majesty's Forces, and sadly two were killed on active service. In 1940, the Club adopted H.M.T. Cape Melville. Correspondence was kept with the crew, and parcels of knitted garments and cigarettes were sent, until the ship was destroyed by enemy action in 1942.

*Gladys and Charlie Middleton
with YFC stock at
the first Club Sale in
the Spring of 1938 at
East Budleigh Market.*

above:
A well attended YFC stock show in the 1930's.

below:
Gordon Hallett, left, and his brother
Leonard with YFC stock 1938.

Gladys Midddleton, George and Archie Smith and Percy Baker
at the first Show and Sale 1938.

In 1943 it was decided to invite members of the Women's Land Army to become honourary Club members due to the fact that active service had depleted the numbers. During the War years a large sum of money was raised for the Red Cross and the Women's Land Army Benevolent Fund. Altogether in 1943 £114.10s.2d. was raised.

In the Exeter Group Public Speaking Competitions the Club teams were winners in 1944, 45, 46, 49, 51. Not a bad record!

In the Group Drama competition, the YFC was placed 2nd. in both 1951 and 1952. The Club, which started at a very high level, has maintained this throughout the years.

Drama was quite an important part of the YFC learning curve.

Group drama competitions were held annually, and the Club members put their backs into making a good production.

This picture was taken in the Public Hall in 1959, before a very discerning and well dressed audience!

The picture on the right shows Florence Fisher, Brenda Hallett and Brenda Pyne at a poultry trussing class in 1951.

The picture on the left shows a cheesemaking class at Webbers Farm, also in 1951.
Left to right back row: *Hazel Broom, Joan Sellick, Brenda Broom.*
Front row: *Florence Fisher, Pam Lee, Miss Lloyd (DCC Instructress), Brenda Hallett and Dorothy Freemantle.*

above: *Poultry judging class*
left: *Rope making class at Courtbrook Farm.*

YFC Sheep shearing classes in 1939 used hand shears before the days of electricity.

Left:
Ploughing was obviously a very important part of agricultural life. At local ploughing matches competition was strong, and Tom Broom from Courtbrook Farm, Clyst St. George, is seen here competing in 1951.

Right::
Stock judging classes at Lower Cooks Farm, Woodbury Salterton in 1951-2.

This superb picture of a YFC Stock Judging class was taken at Gulliford Farm in 1946.
Those present were from left to right: *Tom Mortimer, Norman White, Mrs WB Hallett, Arthur Channon, Sam Miller, Harold Roberts, John Hill, A Pink, WB Hallett, B Crowe, George Pyne, Pat Glanvill (now Bowles), Rob Pyne, John Glanvill of Bagmores, Harry Stokes, Bertie Stamp, ?, Norman Bowles, Basil Palmer, Ralph Bowditch, Gordon Hallett, Gerald Fisher, Eileen Hawkins, Enid Tavender, Eileen Parsons, Doreen Tavender, Jack Tavender, and John Hocken, then County Secretary of the YFC movement.*

The picture on the left shows the members of the YFC at their Silver Jubilee AGM in 1962 in the Village Hall. Since then of course in 1987 they have celebrated their Golden Jubilee. George Daw, the President is seen in the centre, along with many other well known faces.

During the whole of the period members have always been forward thinking and ready for a challenge. In the late 1960's John Smith, then of Cottles Farm, was awarded a scholarship for a nine month trip to Australia to study farming. Pat West, a town girl from Exeter joined the Club in the sixties, and considers it was the best thing she has ever done. In spite of all the talk about it being a marriage bureau, Pat is still a single girl!

Woodbury has had many prominent and forward thinking people in positions of authority during the Century, and since 1937 a fair share of them have come up through the Young Farmers Club movement, where in particular they learned the art of public speaking. This has always stood them in good stead for life's battles ahead.

It is not possible to name all of them, and tell their stories, as it would probably fill the book alone, and they have all done a good job during their periods of office. However, I have decided to take as an example the most recent, as he is still fresh in people's minds. His name is John H Glanvill. He was "born young", as they say in farming circles, but since then he has achieved a lot.

above:
John Glanvill pictured at the age of 3 years, with his sister June aged 4.

right:
Still a pair, both are now at a more useful age.

After work on the farm, John (2nd. right) could be seen at the YFC public speaking contests, with Brenda Hallett, Leonard Hallett and his other sister Pat, having won the contest and brought home the cups.

John was Chairman of the Woodbury YFC in 1952 and since then he has been Chairman of the Devon Branch of the National Farmers Union, and later held National positions within that organisation for many years. In the 1990's he was elected to East Devon District Council to represent Woodbury and surrounding parishes, and concurrently to Devon County Council, where in 1997 he became Chairman. He is also a member of the Devon & Cornwall Police Authority. A lifetime of public service in between farming at Rydon. **All in all a fitting tribute to an early training in the Woodbury Young Farmers Club system.**

The High Sheriff of Devon, Lady Clinton, with her husband Lord Clinton, John Glanvill and his wife Dorothy, welcome the Queen to Exeter in 1998.

John Glanvill, Chairman Devon County Council 1997 - 1998.

The Flowershow and Gymkhana

The Village has always been very competitive in the growing of produce, whether it be flowers or vegetables. From the 1920's until the early 1950's an annual produce show was staged in the field to the north of Oakhayes Lane where it meets the main Exeter road. Ultimately the field became known as "Flowershow Field". Later, when the Cricket Club took over an area here it became known as "The Cricket Field". Now of course there is a new cricket field.

To make a full day of entertainment a gymkhana was added to the proceedings, and this became part of a circuit of gymkhanas put on within the district. I am led to believe that one certain gentleman was a good show jumper, and he would try to get to as many shows in one day to win as many prizes as possible. A little like the modern jockey, but without the helicopter! Ultimately, other more amateur riders became a little dismayed.

George Daw of Sandyhills is pictured with his daughter Miss Patience (Patsy) Daw at a show in 1923, with band behind.

above:
At the 1923 Show a formidable array of produce is to be seen in the large marquee.

right:
On the same day, jumping in progress with a large crowd watching.
The trees of "Oakhayes" corner form the backdrop.

And pictured again here with some of his superb produce, and his daughter Joan, now Mrs Joan Sangwin.

At the prizegiving in 1940 Bill Summerfield was the "Champion". Out of 37 entries he won 15 firsts, 14 seconds and 4 thirds!

Below are three pictures reproduced from newspapers, and not of such good quality. They have been included as they are part of the record.

The winning male and female riders being congratulated by the judge.

above:
Mr George Daw again in 1940, now Chairman of the Show, with Mrs Chattock from Oakhayes, who was crowning the Queen Marie Sellick.

left:
Part of the large assembled crowd.

The Women's Institute

The Women's Institute, better known as the WI, was formed in Woodbury in 1920. It has been a strong organisation ever since, and had a similar criteria to that of the Young Farmers Club - the education of its members in everyday attributes. From the preparation and preservation of food, dressmaking and all activities revolving around the home, the WI has also been involved in the drama scene, putting on plays at regular intervals in the Public Hall, as it was in the 50's. My own mother was deeply involved in the movement during this middle years period, and I well remember our house being an extension of the Hall for the rehearsal of plays, and for the putting together of the costumes for the same.

The WI motto, "For Home and Country", aptly captures the spirit of the organisation, particularly in the years after the War. A new generation of women was emerging, who, like the YFC, sought knowledge and improved methods for their daily life.

One particular lady who stands out from the crowd was Miss Blanche Fulford, from the Priory, who was a founder member of the Woodbury Institute in 1920, and was its first Honourary Secretary. The following year she was elected to the County Federation which had just been formed, and was its first County Secretary, a post she held for 25 years. On her retirement in 1946 she was presented with a beautifully hand scribed book, the text of which is featured below.

MISS BLANCHE FULFORD has been connected with the Women's Institute Movement in Devon from its very earliest days.

When the County Federation came into being in 1920 she was appointed on the Committee, and in November 1921 she was elected County Secretary in which capacity she has served ever since.

When she took on the County Secretaryship among the Institutes already in existence were Cullompton, Cornwood and Alphington, and in February 1920 when an Institute was formed at Woodbury Miss Fulford was elected its first Honorary Secretary.

By the summer of 1920 there were twenty Women's Institutes in Devon, among which were Exmouth Centre, Holcombe Burnell, Sidford, Bridestowe, East Budleigh and

Lympstone, and later, Princetown, Hawkchurch, Littleham and Tipton St. John formed their Institutes; to be followed by Lydford, North Petherwin and Walkhampton, the latter being dissolved in 1922.

Miss Fulford has seen the Movement grow from this small beginning until the present day when there are two hundred and thirty-three Institutes in Devon.

She has worked as a County Organiser as well as Secretary to the Devon Federation, and in addition she has undertaken the work in connection with the Secretaryship of the Women's Institutes' Organisation Sub-Committee, dealing with the organisation of new Institutes in the County, arranging for Voluntary County Organisers to attend meetings of the older Institutes, and arranging speakers' tours in Devon, all of which has entailed a very great deal of work.

She has been a staunch and unfailing friend of the Movement in this County, and the Women's Institutes of Devon acknowledge with sincere gratitude her valuable services throughout the past twenty-five years and unite in wishing her many years of happiness in her retirement from her official duties.

Miss Blanche Fulford in 1952.

This picture of the WI taken on Oakhayes Lawn in the late 1920's shows the full strength of the movement. Mrs Chattock, owner of Oakhayes is seen front row left, with Miss Blanche Fulford fifth left.

The same Miss Blanche Fulford is seen here again in 1952, planting a tree presented by the WI to commemorate the Coronation of Queen Elizabeth II. Harry Stokes is holding the tree.

THE MIDDLE YEARS

The WI were always regular entrants in the Woodbury Carnivals, and one of their floats is seen here in Webbers Farm yard before joining the procession.
Just look at those wheels on the wagon!

below:
A competition entry in 1961, which attained 1st. prize. The backcloth was painted by Margaret Sellek, handbells by Kathleen Stokes, sallys by Mrs Heal and hessian covered boxes by Judith Sellek.

above:
the WI in the 1950's.

right:
The Woodbury WI pictured celebrating the Golden Jubilee of the Women's Institute Movement in 1970. Since then of course another 25 years has passed.

The Sixty Plus Club

The 60 Plus Club was formed in 1959, and from looking through the photographic record that has been kept of its activities throughout the years, it is quite clear that although passing through the dreaded age barrier of 60 years, the members of the Club certainly could not be classed as "over the hill"!

They have been most energetic in their pursuits, have enjoyed annual outings and entered into competitions with great success, and even been caught up in unforeseen incidents involving army tanks!

Their photo albums have a two fold value to Woodbury folk, as they have recorded not just the activity side of things, but also they have captured the faces of many old village residents who are sadly no longer with us. This of course gives us a good opportunity to take a look at "Middle Years" people later on in the book, along with a few others as well.

The picture on the left was taken in 1959 shortly after the club's inception.

The picture on the right shows the Club as winners of the Handicraft Exhibition, for the affiliated clubs of the Exeter and District group.

Pictured are from left to right:
Evelyn Hopkinson, Margaret Sellek, Betty Ferris, ? Galliver, Hetty Moore and Elsie Smith.

left:
On an outing to Weymouth in 1959.
***left to right:** Mesdames Norton, ?, ?, Gooding, Alsopp.*

right:
On a visit to Ilfracombe in 1960.
left to right:
Mesdames Henley, Westaway, Wheaton, Turner, Moore.

right:
Dartmouth 1961.
left to right:
Mesdames Davey, Alsopp, Govier, Norton.

left:
Butlins at Minehead in 1966.
left to right:
Mesdames Salter, Boyland, ?, Norton, Ferris.

In 1963 the Club outing was to be to Bournemouth. This was not to be without some unscheduled excitement as the press cutting below describes. However, many had probably been through two world wars, and this was not going to dampen their enthusiasm! Someone even hopped out and took a photo!

60+ CLUB IN TANK "HOLD-UP"

Fifty seven members of Woodbury Sixty Plus Club, travelling in two coaches to Bournemouth on Tuesday for their annual summer outing, were held up for two hours near Chideock, Dorset, when an Army lorry with a tank on board slewed across the road. Traffic was halted for some distance in both directions.

"But nobody minded", said Club president and organiser, Mrs B. Ferris, "and for the whole two hours we sat and sang songs. In fact we sang till we were hoarse".

below: Gordon Ferris (headmaster) and his wife Betty, both staunch supporters of the club, being presented with a gift by Mrs Norton on the occasion of their Silver Wedding, 1967.

above:
A Honiton Lace collar made by Mrs Reg Newton's grandmother (seen inset making it), which was exhibited at one of the handicraft exhibitions.

right:
The Christmas Party in 1967.

The Scout Troop

I am not entirely sure when the Woodbury Scout Troop was formed, but the earliest pictures currently at hand date from the 1940's, and feature several residents of the Village who are "still around"!

The Club has always had a bit of a "hand to mouth" existence, as finding leaders has never been easy. However, many Village children have been through the system, which still exists today.

This is the earliest picture of the Scouts that I have, which I would date around 1945. The hut was situated in Town Lane, where "Long Summers" now stands.
Back row left to right: *Dave Sellick, Derek Channon, Peter Morris, Ken Lang, Dick Yorke, Percy Pollard, Percy Heather (Scoutmaster).*
Middle row: *Peter Loman, Stan Bowden, Alec Pollard, Dave Jones, ?, ?.*
Front row: *Raymond Bray, ?, Edwin Bamsey, ?, Ken Radford, Michael Worley, ?.*

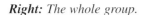

Left:
This picture and the one below were taken at the Woodbury Scout Group Camp at Gilwell Park in London in 1953.
Featured from left:
Back Row: *Jason Marks, Lewis Cornish, Raymond Sellick, Twinkle Bamsey, Eric Sansom.*
Front row: *Ivor Loman, Victor Fox, Whippy Smeath.*

Right: *The whole group.*

from left back row: Bill Loman (ASL), Raymond Sellick, Eric Sansom, Clifford Marks, Jason Marks, Albert (Twinkle) Bamsey, Lewis Cornish (SL).

Middle row: *Ron Miller, Ken Sellick, Peter Burden, Ivor Loman, Victor Fox.*

Front row: *Geoffrey Gallagher, ? White, Bobby Miller, David Ellis, Anthony (Whippy) Smeath, and Malcolm Hitchcock.*

93

Football and Other Clubs

Woodbury has always been fond of its football, and in my early days the Club ground was in Woodmanton Lane, just up from Higher Venmore Farm. Subsequently it was relocated to the new Woodbury Playing Field when it was acquired from the Rolle Estate. Photographs of the Club's early days are scant, but what I have is featured here. There must have been some unrest at some stage, as a breakaway club was formed at Woodmanton for a period.

The School also seemed to be into football in 1926, as the picture below records. Through the years Salterton has also had a strong football following.

The Woodbury team in 1921.

The Woodmanton team in the 1940's.

The School team in 1926, according to the date written on the ball!

Other Club pictures

At risk of being told that I have left someone out, I must repeat what I said at the beginning of the book. That is, that this photographic record is not intended to be a concise history of the Parish, but a review of those photographs that have been made available to me. In modern day parlance this could be described as "What you see is what I've got"! It is impossible to research every organisation within the time scale available, but I hope that what has been printed gives a reasonable view of what has been going on over the years in the Woodbury social scene. A few more assorted pictures follow, to round off this section.

The Skittle Club

Some of the founder members of the Woodbury Skittle Club, pictured here in the 1950's.
From left to right they are: *Stan Bowden, Bill Huxtable, Bert Skinner, Frank Bowden, Alan Middleton, Charlie Middleton and Frank Miller.*
They built the Maltsters Arms skittle alley.

The Cork Club

Members of the Men's Cork Club pictured on the Arch c.1950.
The picture contains a lot of familiar faces to older Woodbury residents.
All names are known, but too many to list here!

The Royal British Legion

The British Legion were strong in the Village following the War years, and are seen here marching past the Maltsters to celebrate the ending of the 1939-45 War, with Bob Fox bearing the standard. For obvious reasons, numbers have now depleted.

The Tennis Club

*Woodbury Lawn Tennis Club members 1959. They were the winners of the Weaver Trophy. **Left to right standing are:** Peggy Hart, Dick Hart, Mrs Jarman, John Vicary, Eric Ware, Joan Vickery, ?, Joan Ware, Ann Marks, Aileen Walton, Muriel Hallett. **Front row:** Ron Hallett, Geoff Smith, John Bassett, Harry Jarman, Joy Bassett, Betty Baker.*
This photo was taken on the old grass court in the playing field. Prior to this court being laid, the club previously played where Park Way now stands.

Agriculture around Woodbury

Until the recent blows to the farming industry during the 1980's and 90's, agriculture was the major industry of the area, and the largest employer. The majority of village people had some connection with the land, either by working on it directly or by having a family member employed on a farm. I remember my father saying that when he started his farming career at Webbers Farm in 1932, around 15 people were employed there in some degree or other. At the time of his death only one full time employee remained. The fall in numbers was largely due to increased efficiency and advances in mechanisation from the 50's onwards. Increased wages for farmworkers did not help during periods of extreme uncertainty, of which there were many, and savings had to be made. Of course these periods still exist today, and are even more aggravated by the country's membership of the EEC, whereby no-one is accountable for anything, and the true facts of any situation are not wanted to be heard. The following pictures however, depict a more genuine period of time when following the 1939-45 War, everyone pulled together for the common good.

Sows and litters roam in Bonfire Lane in the 1940's, on their way to the Pathfields. There was little traffic then, so the pigs were left to their own devices.

Jack Nash's, now Haymans butchers shop, can be seen in the background.

The author's father tending his Large Black sows and piglets behind the Roundhouse at Webbers Farm in 1941.

The Roundhouse was a building where a horse went round and round in harness. This in turn, via gears, drove belts and pulleys to power grain grinding machinery of the time.

The Roundhouse has now of course gone, to be replaced by somewhat squarer ones!

During the early part of this period the main form of transport was the pony and trap. Seen here are the two young Glanvill girls, June and Pat, outside Rydon Farm.

This form of transport continued until the late 1950's on many farms, and I remember that Reggie Newton who farmed at Rushmore Farm, below Woodbury Castle, came to the village daily in his until he retired in 1960.

Percy Stediford, seen here behind Siddons, also had a shire horse which was used for ploughing in the fields, and pulling the heavy wagons.

Walter Chapman was the horseman at Webbers Farm during my early years, and I have memories of being sat on top of the carthorse pictured here, and being told to "Hang on"!

The picture is taken outside the stable and the horsetrough can be seen in the background, and the cobbled yard below the horse's feet. The stable at the time was cobbled also.

Emanuel Hawkins is seen here raking up hay.

One horse was used for most jobs, but for ploughing it was customary to work with a pair. The pair had to be well matched so that one did not go faster than the other.

Bringing in the harvest was a laborious job, where many hands made light work.

At Lower Mallocks Farm they too had their draft horse "Blossom", who was looked after by both Walt Gooding (above), and Harry Miller (below).

Fortunately or unfortunately, I can remember as far back as these days! It was quite often the job of the younger members of the family to have to "make the load", as they were not usually big enough, or strong enough to pitch the sheaves up on to the wagon. This was not an easy job, as sheaves came up from all directions. The sheaves were not square like modern bales, but conical in shape therefore difficult to stack evenly. They were also very slippery, and had to be stacked each side of the wagon with the heads facing inwards. The whole wagon and load bounced across the field, stopping when surrounded by sheaves on the ground which were duly loaded.

Loads were inclined to become lop sided whilst under construction, which was a fatal error, and on many an occasion I can remember shortly after putting the last sheaves on the top the whole load would slip off and had to be loaded all over again. If nothing else, one soon learned to do the job properly the first time. However, you were not properly "initiated" until disaster had struck at least once!

TWENTIETH CENTURY WOODBURY

During the War years, Woodbury had its share of Landgirls, and one such called Kathleen Champion was stationed at Webbers Farm. Food production was on the increase and extra help was needed. Many men had gone to War so the Landgirls filled the gap.

Throughout this period, and up to the early 1950's it was common for most farms to kill their own livestock for home consumption. Before the days of humane killers, pigs were strung up to a beam by the nose and their throats were cut.

At that time Jack Sellick was the area "executioner", and he is seen in the picture below with Kathleen Champion following such an event. The Landgirl was obviously being "initiated" into country life by being given the pig's head as a trophy! Following this the meat would be taken off and made into brawn which was delicious. The rest of the carcase would be salted or smoked, and the intestines eaten as chitlings, a delicacy that was worth waiting for! Jack Sellick finished his time in life as Sexton of the Church, a parallel there somewhere!

*Landgirl Kathleen Champion, **left,** with Jack Sellick, and **above,** Landgirl Ann Blackledge (later Pidsley).*

Above:
*George Wilson, with Frank Turner, Jack Grant and Edna and Fred Neil pitching sheaves of corn onto a rick in 1941, and **right,** in a more recently posed picture showing how hay was cut with a scythe in the 40's.*

THE MIDDLE YEARS

Harry and Kathleen Stokes, the author's parents, are seen here in Bonfire Lane in 1940 (before the author was born!), with their trap pulled by the pony called "Ginger".

My father recalls a story when he was driving the trap to Blackhill, and as he was about to go up the hill at Ford Water the pony stopped dead in its tracks and would not move despite all attempts.
Seconds later a large tree fell right across the road in front of them!

However, things were about to move on from these sleepy days of farming, to a more mechanised era. Tractors and machinery were being imported from America, which would help to produce more food with greater ease. Earlier tractors c.1937 only had iron wheels, the rear ones known as "spade lugs". These had to have steel bands applied to them before they could go on the road, otherwise they dug up the surface. Later, rubber tyres were introduced, which made life a lot easier.

However, a disaster of monumental proportions was about to strike at Webbers Farm completely out of the blue, which the press cutting beside graphically describes.

At that time it was the only case in the whole country, and its reasons for striking, as always, are not apparent. As in all cases of this nature, it is not possible to restock a farm for a long period of time, following a programme of intense disinfection, therefore the farming pattern had to change for a number of years. The Pathfields saw an unusual crop for a time, anemonies! Two acres were drilled and the resulting output was sent to Covent Garden by train from Woodbury Road Station. It kept the staff employed and generated some income, but when the War came flower growing stopped.

Express & Echo
· TUESDAY, JUNE 8th. 1937

WOODBURY'S ORDEAL BY FIRE.

Anyone who did not know what was happening at Woodbury last night might have thought that a swailing was going on. Into the evening sky rose dense volumes of smoke which spread itself like a shroud of mourning over the district. And well it might, for that smoke came from such a crematorium as it has not seen before.

* * *

Heartbreaking to Mr Harry Stokes it must have been to watch that smoke; to hear the sizzling and cracking in the blazing furnace which belched it forth; and to reflect that into those consuming flames were being hurled the entire stock of his farm. Altogether 235 animals on Webbers farm, and one or two more besides, received the sentence of death during the weekend. Almost with the regularity and the monotony of a machine gun, humane killers did their dread work, so that by tonight there will be a strange silence brooding over hitherto smiling acres where grazed 54 bullocks, 131 sheep and about 50 swine in turn grunted and snored.

* * *

Only a farmer can realise what that means; this sudden and terrible end to years of hard work and planning and hoping. Compensation there may be, but no money can fully compensate when calamity of this kind befalls. Yet so dread a disease is Foot and Mouth, so mysterious in its origin, and so difficult to keep within bounds, that apparently only this most distressing ordeal of death and destruction by fire can cope with it. It is sad to think that until some long looked for discovery is made, there seems to be no satisfactory alternative.

Above:
Cutting corn with the binder and
Standard Fordson tractor in the
Pathfields 1937.

Right:
Jack Grant at Salterton sweeping in
hay with an Allis Chalmers Model
B tractor in 1940.

John Stamp with his little cousin (the author) in 1943
cultivating in Cottles Lane.
Winsor House and Jubilee House can be seen in the
background.

Tractors went from all iron wheels to having rubbers on
the back and eventually all rubber tyres.
The rear rubbers alleviated the need to put bands on for
road travel.

The Pyne family from Postlake Farm at harvest time
c.1940.

THE MIDDLE YEARS

Throughout the 1940's and 50's four herds of cows used to traverse the village every day. There was Havill's from Higher Venmore, Stamp's from Woodbury House, Norton's from Cornishes and the ones pictured here from Stokes's at Webbers. Every so often all would meet on this corner of Bonfire Lane. When such an unfortunate occurrence took place, the cows made a certain noise which is easily recognised by a farmer as "trouble".
If having breakfast at Webbers and the noise was heard, one shot out into the road to try to keep them apart!

Right:
Hay and corn was stored in large ricks, usually in a field near the main farmstead.
As the ricks were high, some method had to be found to get it to the top. Seen here is a "Pole Elevator", which consisted of two poles of wood erected upwards and held in place by stays. The commodity was tipped in a heap as shown and a grab would be lowered on to it. A horse would then be driven forwards, raising the grab as it went. When at the right level it would be swung in over the rick and the load deposited on top. If it was corn, a threshing machine would arrive later to harvest the grain. Pole elevators were later replaced by mechanical ones, although still horse driven.

However, after a hard day's haymaking, what better way to relax and enjoy yourself. This picture shows a hound puppy show in action, with a large crowd in 1940.

It was customary for farms to take one or two puppies from the East Devon Hunt, and "walk" them. That is to bring them up until they were ready to be introduced into the hunt for the next season.
It was a great honour to have produced the best puppy.

Evacuees to Woodbury

Just prior to the commencement of the 1939-45 war, the Government decided that for safety's sake young children should be evacuated from the built up areas of England's major cities. This was a highly organised exercise which brought several of these children to our village.

Most of them were only seven or eight years old when removed from their parents homes to be billeted with our village families, which must have been quite an experience for them. Most had never been outside the city before, let alone away from home, and country life was to be an enormous culture shock for them.

However, they were taken in and looked after as if they were an existing family member. They went to school here and joined in the local activities, and some are featured in the early picture of the Scouts on page 93.

Visits back home were rare, and many came to like the country scene so well that after the War ended they stayed on to become "fully fledged" villagers. Two of the most notable examples are Reggie Brown and Joan Blackall (later to become Sellick). Joan eventually married Trixie, and lived in Woodbury until her death. Reggie moved away for a period to follow his career, but on his retirement could not resist returning to live here.

Left:
Reggie Brown pictured in 1999, a far cry from his earlier photo at the bottom of the page.

Right:
Joan Sellick, pictured at Haydon's Cottage c.1980.

Left:
Evacuees Alan Hann and Derek Moreland pondering their thoughts sitting on the gate at Higher Venmore Farm c.1940.

Below:
Joan Sellick as many would have known her. A self sufficient person with a heart of gold. Always a Cockney, her views were always forthright!

Left: left to right
Reggie Brown and Derek Moreland (both evacuees) with local lads Roy Allsop, Terry Allsop and Ken Allsop c.1940.

The Royal Marines

The Royal Marine camp at Exton, although normally called Lympstone, was set up in 1938 prior to the start of the 1939-45 war. Its aim then, and now, was for the initial training of Royal Marine recruits. It has been an integral part of Woodbury parish since then, and through the years has provided considerable employment to local civilians.

Its main training ground has been on Woodbury Common, following on from the days of the Devon Infantry Yeomanry, but its mode of operation has been somewhat different to the latter. Helicopters have replaced horses, and mechanised vehicles have replaced the carts.

Since the early days of wooden huts it has been continuously improved to become a state of the art training centre with all the modern facilities that go with it.

The pictures on this page were taken in the 1950's, when the camp's accommodation was wooden huts for all ranks.

A young Duke of Edinburgh is seen carrying out an inspection on one occasion, and at another time it is being done by the Commander in Chief, Plymouth.

Both visit the Common to view training activities there.

Photos on this page courtesy of The Western Morning News Co.

During a water shortage in 1952, the Royal Marines help out with a bowser in Parkway.

Mid-Century People

Albert Hoile came to Woodbury in 1936 when he retired from a lifetime career in the Devon Constabulary. He took up the position of Master of the Remand Home in Globe House and his wife became the Matron. He moved away to Pinhoe early in 1939 just before war was declared, and in November of that year the Remand Home was closed down. It was subsequently turned into a home for unmarried mothers. During his service in the Police force he was one of only 10 constables in the whole of England to be receive the medal of King George V and Queen Mary's Silver Jubilee - awarded because he was in the service when they came to the throne and still in it at their Silver Jubilee. His daughters, Betty Spurgeon and Ruby Hitchcock, still live in the village.

The George V and Queen Mary Silver Jubilee medal awarded to Albert Hoile.

Following the demise of the Woodbury Petty Sessional Court in 1918, the Court House, which had been the centre of justice in the parish for over half a century, subsequently had a number of uses like the ones mentioned above.

The old Globe Inn is seen arrowed in the background. Prior to the Court House being built in 1860-61, the Globe was used for all the magistrate's sittings.

Percy and Vera Stediford in their later years. They were always the "life and soul" of any party during their lifetime in the village.

Ida Marks on the left and Mrs Miller. Ida lived in Castle Cottages, and Mrs Miller by the Fire Station.

Above: Mr & Mrs Reg Brewer who lived at the top end of Castle Cottages.
Below: Mr & Mrs Westaway from Salterton.

Above: Mr & Mrs Mabbett who lived opposite the Old Bakery. Mr Mabbett repaired shoes.
Below left: "Mr Henry", an Indian servant, who came back with the Templers from India.

Above: Mr & Mrs Sid Gooding who lived at 5, Gillbrook Cottages.
Below left: Mrs Ledmond, whose house by the Church was washed away in the 1960 floods.
Below right: Reggie & Maud Newton, who farmed at Rushmoor Farm until 1960.

TWENTIETH CENTURY WOODBURY

Of course all of these chaps were also "Mid Century People". They were the Woodbury Home Guard and did their bit for the cause during the 1939 - 45 War. They are pictured here in "The Lawn" with the Church tower behind.

WOODBURY PLATOON

Back Row, Left to Right—L/Cpl. Gooding, Pte. Morrish, Pte. Baker, Pte. Down, Pte. Bowles, Pte. Blackmore, Pte. Miller, Pte. Brewer, Pte. Goss, Pte. Skinner, Pte Yeo, L/Cpl. Jarman
2nd Row, Left to Right—Pte. Palmer, Pte. Stamp, Pte. Baker, Pte. Tucker, Pte. Stubbs, Pte. Auton, Pte. Edworthy, Pte. Hawkins, Pte. Ridler, L/Cpl. Middleton, Pte. Williams, Pte. Sharland
3rd Row, Seated—L/Cpl. Boyland. Cpl. Wilson, Sgt. Smith (G), Sgt. Gallienne. Sgt. Loman, Lt. Rickeard, Lt. Pavey, Q.M.S. Chattock, Sgt. Tapley, Sgt. Hollet, Cpl. Smith (A), Cpl. Marks,
Pte. Reeves (D.R.), Pte. Armstrong, Pte. Sellick, Pte. Marks, Pte. Newton, Pte. Hitchcock. Pte. Bamsey, Pte. Chapman, Pte. Radford, Pte. Hawkins (G), Pte. Pavey (D.R.)

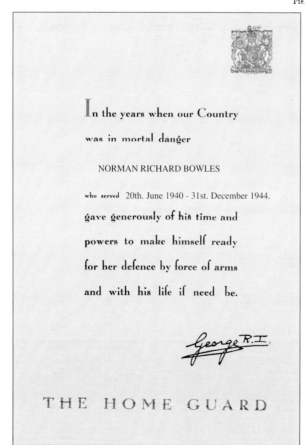

In the years when our Country

was in mortal danger

NORMAN RICHARD BOWLES

who served 20th. June 1940 - 31st. December 1944.

gave generously of his time and

powers to make himself ready

for her defence by force of arms

and with his life if need be.

George R.I.

THE HOME GUARD

At the end of their service all of these brave men also received a citation from the King, and a War Medal for the defence of their country.

The School Case

In July 1947 a most unusual situation occurred in the Village, and notices like the one beside were put up to summon villagers to a meeting in the Public Hall. The whole scenario was brought about by parents of children at the Woodbury School, who were extremely unhappy with the methods of teaching that were going on at the time. Things reached such a state by the 24th. June 1947, when a particular incident occurred between the Headmaster and one of the lady teachers, that the parents decided to take a course of action which would probably involve the removal of the Headmaster.

A petition was drawn up and signed by a large number of people, and forwarded to the Education Authority. However, the Headmaster took exception to the wording of the petition, and its method of production, and instigated a libel, slander and conspiracy suit against them. This was contested in June 1948 and lasted five days in the County Court. It attracted national newspaper coverage during its course, due to its unusual content.

NOTICE.

A number of Parents who are concerned about their Children's Education have complained by Petition to the County Education Authority.

In order to ascertain the views of the Ratepayers and Parishioners on the matter, it is proposed to hold an Open MEETING on WEDNESDAY, 16th July, at the PUBLIC HALL, WOODBURY, at 8·30 p.m., to consider the whole matter.

Anyone who is interested in the subject is invited to attend with the object of expressing their views.

Right: The Headmaster Mr C H Kinsman and his wife attending the Court.

Mr Justice Humphreys The presiding Judge.

Miss Phillips, the infant teacher, who it was alleged had been in various quarrels with Mr Kinsman, and could not continue.

It was alleged that Mr Kinsman was a bully both to the other lady teachers and to the children. Children, including girls, were caned excessively for minor offences, and often went home bleeding.

Statements from various witnesses said that the children were made to do menial tasks for the Headmaster and his wife, during normal periods of tuition. These included going around the village collecting pig swill, gathering acorns, walking the dog and gardening. In evidence, one child said he was punished for killing a cat, which he had not done. Another said he was beaten four or five times a week, and kicked through a door into another classroom, which was corroborated by both teachers and children. Girls were made to bend down and touch their toes whilst corporal punishment was administered, and major rows took place between the Headmaster and the lady teachers in front of the children of 7- 8 years of age, bringing them to tears. Mr Kinsman who had been Headmaster since 1935, lost his case and was subsequently dismissed from his post.

Parents and children outside the County Court.

The Later years
The 1960 Floods

One of the first major happenings for this period was the floods of October 1960. This left Woodbury and Exton in a particularly devastated state. The whole area of Devon was badly hit, and many parts had 2.9 inches of rain in three hours. This was the culmination of a three week period of atrocious weather, during which the village had been flooded four times. Water rushed down Castle Lane and Cottles Lane from the Common, much of it coming from waterlogged fields. The normally quiet stream that crosses the road at the base of Bonfire Hill turned into a raging torrent, burst its banks and overflowed by the Fire Station. This water tore around by the Church, undermining Mrs Ledmond's cob cottage, which was completely destroyed. This stood where the small car park now is between the White Hart and the Green. Many buildings were flooded in the lower reaches of the village.

A rather fuzzy picture taken of the torrent of water passing around the Church wall towards the White Hart. There was little time to stand firm!

In Castle Lane the water was the full width of the road, bringing stones and debris with it. The debris eventually blocked drains and culverts further down, which stopped the water going on its proper course.

left:
Sid Marks the Cobbler views the damage to his house Beech Cott, in Gillbrook, which was directly on top of the culvert, and water came up through the floor causing severe damage.

The road at Ford Water, which had been under repair from the previous week's flood, was more severely damaged and had to be shored up to prevent more of it falling in, due to the constant stream of water.

Things were so severe that the M.P. for Honiton, Mr Robert Mathew (second from right), came to inspect the scene. He is seen here with Devon County Council, St. Thomas Rural District Council and Parish Council officials inspecting the damage.

Both pictures on this page reproduced from newsprint.

M.P. SENT FLOODING S.O.S. TO MINISTER

The Minister was told by Mr HG Stokes, Chairman of the Parish Council, and by fellow councillors, that on Wednesday morning the 19th. October water swept down Church Road, through the White Hart Hotel and into the main village road. Houses in Gillbrook were flooded again as the culvert which runs at the back of them overflowed.

Mr Roy Medlen, licensee of the White Hart described the floods of this week as more frightening than last time. Among others who were seriously affected were Mr Norman Joy, Fred Goodwin and Mrs Skinner, all of whom were flooded recently.

County Police diverted traffic over Woodbury Common, when the second flood again damaged Ford Water, making it unsafe.

Early on Friday, (21st. October), DCC workmen erected a sandbag barricade along 50 yards of the bank of the culvert towards Gillbrook, to protect houses which had already been flooded four times in three weeks. After his visit, Mr Mathew sent a telegram to the Minister of Housing asking for authority for work to be started which would prevent a recurrence of the flooding.

TWENTIETH CENTURY WOODBURY

Exton also received a pasting at the hands of the elements during this three week period, and the old cob Church of St. Andrews was washed away by flood waters on 30th. September 1960. People who live in Exton will well know that all water that passes through Woodbury village ultimately also passes through Exton before it discharges into the River Exe, plus more that is picked up en route.

The Church was totally destroyed, and an appeal for £11,000 was raised for its rebuilding. This unique building, which had a thatched roof as well as its cob walls, had been used as a tithe barn since the 15th Century. It had been given for use as a Church by Lady Rolle in 1864, and had become an invaluable part of village life.

St. Andrews Church Exton before disaster struck.

After the event a sorry sight.

Five hundred years of life, which by an Act of God and the elements, was consigned to history in one day!

God moves in mysterious ways!

Picture courtesy the Express & Echo.

The new St. Andrews is seen here under construction in 1963.

The old cottages seen in the picture above, which belonged to the Rolle Estate, were demolished. The land on which they stood was given by the estate for the re-building of the Church.

The Wind of Change

Up until the late 1950's, Woodbury had been a place where the population was largely indigenous. Everyone knew everyone, and all jobs were mainly local. But with the advent of better forms of transport, new roads and motorways, distances to other places became less. I remember as a boy that a journey to Bristol was almost a two day event in an old Bradford van, and London was entertained only on special occasions. Now Bristol can be driven to in about one hour, and London in three hours.

This of course meant that jobs could be held at greater distances. The converse therefore also applied, and as Exeter was a major centre with its university, banks, insurance and legal facilities, along with Government offices which were expanding at an enormous rate, people were being "imported" from other parts of the country to fill these posts.

Woodbury, in tandem with most other villages in a 10 to 15 mile radius, therefore had to expand to cope with the influx. Up until then only a minor number of new properties were built every year, but this was to change! In the mid 50's Summerfield was built, an estate of 40 bungalows. This was followed in the early 60's by Longmeadow and Longpark two other large bungalow estates. By being bungalows, this also encouraged a large influx of "upcountry" people of retirement age.

The area for development in the late 1950's and early 1960's was in this area. Summerfield is seen at the left, with Longpark in the centre and Longmeadow to the right. First time buyers in Longmeadow bought their two bedroomed properties for £1250.00 and the three bedroomed ones for £1500.00!
At the turn of the Century they are now selling for the best part of £80,000 each! **Photo courtesy of the Express & Echo.**

Prior to the Summerfield development the scene looked like this.
The only dwelling there was the one of William (Bill) Summerfield, who used the area for his geese to roam.

TWENTIETH CENTURY WOODBURY

The next 30 years was to see further major expansion in the house building scene throughout the Parish. The largest which was dubbed "The Golden Heart" was built over a three year period from 1981-84 and had an initial content of 101 dwellings. Controversy was never far away during its construction, which culminated in the erection of the so called "Berlin Wall". This will be dealt with later. The Clinton Devon Estates sold the old Webbers Farm site in the centre of the village in 1983, and that was converted to accommodate 21 new properties.

The Old Webbers Farm development took place in 1984, converting the redundant farm buildings and house, which were built in the 1850's to residential dwellings, and providing the 13 new houses of Culvery Close, seen below.

The "Golden Heart" development of over 100 dwellings started in 1981 and was finished by 1984 in three phases. This still had the Church as a backdrop, but from a different angle.

THE LATER YEARS

Exton was also ripe for development, because of its proximity to Exeter. It's large gardens from days gone by soon became building plots as prices began to rise, and many did not want such large gardens anymore.

Eighteen houses in Barton Close were completed in 1991, followed by 11 at Pratts Nurseries and farm building conversion at Exton Barton. Exton's beautiful waterfront (below), must have been quite an attraction for prospective buyers.

Like any other village the new skyline soon became dominated by the rooves of new dwellings, initially looking a little stark, but eventually blending in by a process of ageing and tree planting.

The picture on the right shows a glimpse of Exton in 1994, where the old, the middle and the new all blend well together.

Salterton too could not avoid the developer's eye. Once the first time sewerage programme had been installed in the late 1980's, building commenced. Prior to that there-had been an embargo on development due to insufficient sewerage facilities, which in fact were non existent except for septic tanks.

Since the erection of the 32 houses in New Way between 1951 - 53, the next largest development was the conversion of the old farm buildings at Bridge Farm, which produced another 3 in 1972. Conversion of Cooks

Farm buildings followed in 1989, having been sold by Devon County Council. Cooks Farm had been one of it's former smallholdings which had been tenanted out to "starter farmers". However, during this period small farms were no longer viable, and were either amalga-mated or sold.

Parkhayes, and building on the former Council Depot in Village Road and above, and Sages Lea behind the old garage, followed in tandem throughout the early 90's and have provided another 40 or so dwellings.

The old Cooks Farm buildings are seen here in 1985, before their re-incarnation to dwellings, and below the new development of Sages Lea, for whose building the village garage had to be sacrificed.

Below: the old village garage and Post Office/Shop before demolition in 1989. The replacement Post Office is seen right, although this has now closed down due to lack of support.

The picture on the left *shows the old DCC depot in 1987, which had been a prominent feature of Salterton for many years.*

The picture above *shows the new dwellings which were built over it during 1990-93.*

THE LATER YEARS

Bridge Farm c.1960

Parkhayes c.1970

Webbers Farm c.1980

The "Wind of Change" during the period from 1960 onwards blew through several quarters. Not only was development of the Parish affected by the house building boom, it was also affected by vast changes in the methods of agricultural production. This in general required modern clear span buildings to accommodate larger machinery. Therefore it was probably inevitable that older farmsteads with 100 years old plus buildings would either be demolished, or "preserved" by the developer. The latter at least would leave some record of what went before, like Bridge Farm and Webbers Farm above.

TWENTIETH CENTURY WOODBURY

Because of various Government policies over this later period, and our Country's membership of the EEC, large mountains of various commodities built up in all the countries. England was no exception, and as British agriculture was probably the most efficient of all, large intervention stores had to be built to accommodate grain, beef and all sorts of surplus supplies. Like it or not, Salterton was to be the site for one of these complexes.

Over a period of time Greendale Barton was to be enlarged from a small historic farmstead to acres of concrete and asbestos. Huge lorries roamed the small lanes which had been built for the horse and cart, and considerable antagonism was caused to people living nearby.

Grain silos followed causing dust and smells, which were equally disliked. However, for a period of 10 - 15 years, this complex provided an invaluable asset to the local farming community, by being somewhere near where they could take their produce and more importantly get their grain dried.

As the European Union got their house in order, and reduced subsidies on agricultural produce, these buildings were no longer viable to process purely agricultural products. Now they accommodate activities from concrete block making to Go Cart racing, a far cry from the original concept. However, all that is large is not necessarily without problems, as a fire in the silos showed.

The picture on the right shows one of the large agricultural storage buildings under construction at Greendale Barton in 1987.

The picture on the left shows the finished product. This was one of a complex of many such buildings.

Photo courtesy of the Express & Echo.

Fire appliances are seen here in attendance when internal combustion caused a severe fire within the silo complex in 1989. This took several days to get under control because of the difficulty of access and the toxic gases involved.

Photo courtesy of the Express & Echo

Golf Courses

As the general population became more affluent, membership of golf clubs became a sought after leisure activity. As a direct result of this there soon became an apparent major shortage of golf courses in the Woodbury area. To try to counter this problem, some tried to turn less favoured farmland into courses to meet the demand. In 1971 the Clinton Devon Estates, the landowners of Woodbury Common, applied for planning permission to construct two golf courses on the area of the Common between the Castle and the Royal Marines bombing range. This attracted the wrath of many local people who considered that their rights of access to the Common would be severely diminished or even curtailed. Mr Alan Toyne, a Woodbury resident, who with others formed the "Hands off Woodbury Common Committee" fought hard against this proposal, and the whole issue was forced to a public inquiry. In the end the Secretary of State for the Environment did not give approval for this development to proceed, and it was shelved.

In the late 80's the Carter family were successful in obtaining planning permission to convert Hogsbrook Farm into a golf course, after an equally long and bitter battle with the authorities and local residents. This included permission for a 100 bedroom hotel complex.

Both photos courtesy the Express & Echo.

Alan Toyne, the prime mover of the protest movement, and a dedicated lover of open spaces, is seen here addressing a public meeting at Woodbury Castle on 19th. November 1971. It attracted major television and press coverage at the time.

The picture on the right *shows the Hogsbrook course under construction. Featured in the picture are Brian Miller the General Manager, Bryan Pearson of the course builders and Rowan Carter. They are standing in the hole which was to become the lake at the course.*

In Woodbury Village Hall in September 1994, the Mansell Plans were revealed.

Photo courtesy of the Express and Echo.

In 1994, the Hogsbrook Course came on the market. Amongst those who showed an interest in buying it was Nigel Mansell, the World Champion Formula 1 racing driver. However, a condition of his purchase included getting planning approvals to construct things the way he wanted, along with a large house for himself at the lower end of the complex. What was now the long and familiar route started all over again, each side jockeying for supremacy. Compromises had to be made on all sides, but eventually Mansell obtained sufficient approval to complete the purchase, despite bitter opposition from conservationists.

Since that point, a high class golf course has been constructed along with a superb clubhouse facility - a facility which now serves to the benefit of many local organisations, and allied with it the provision of a considerable number of local jobs. However, Walkidons Way, the most ancient footpath in the Parish, has not come out of the changes unscathed, and is no longer presented in its former glory.

Above:
The new Woodbury Park clubhouse under construction in 1995.

Right:
Walkidons Way in 1984 is seen as an idyllic country lane.

Blackhill Quarry

The quarry at Blackhill was first opened in the early 1930's, and like some of the other things that have happened in "public places" its development has always concerned the conservationists from its inception. Instead of the military just digging small holes in the Common for trenches, the various quarry companies which have operated there have gradually dug larger and larger holes for the extraction of minerals. The Council for the Preservation of Rural England were showing concern about it at their annual meeting in 1938, as seen in the following press cutting.

The Common however, contains the largest deposits of quartzite in the area, which is used for surfacing roads as it is extremely hard. It is even exported as far away as Hampshire.

In the early days everything was done by hand, even the cracking of stone, but since the 1950's mechanisation has taken over, and huge machines are involved in all the processes. The large holes, which are now being backfilled and replanted, have provided most of the building material for post war Exeter and surrounding areas.

"EYESORE" ON WOODBURY COMMON
Plants Spoiled by Sand

Devon C.P.R.E Asked To Take Action

Demand for action over a "growing eyesore" on Woodbury Common, one of East Devon's most popular beauty spots, was made at the annual meeting of the Devon branch of the Council for the Preservation of Rural England.

The matter was asked by Miss F.M. Durham who asked if the Executive Committee had taken any steps against "the large sand pit" on the Common.

"A large part of the Moor is now being covered with sand," she declared, "and many beautiful plants are being spoiled. It is a scar on a lovely piece of the Common, and it is becoming a regular eyesore. Can nothing be done about it?" she asked.

Capt. F.H. Maynard suggested that nothing could be done, unless they could prove that the Common was being enclosed.

The Chairman (Mr. R.B. Phillpotts) assured Miss Durham that the branch had looked into the matter to see if they could register a protest. In view of what she had said, he agreed that they should make further inquiries.

Western Morning News 13th. August 1938.

The picture above was taken in 1968, 30 years after the cutting, and shows washing water being returned to the silt ponds which were the previously excavated areas. Until about this period the holes kept appearing, but environmental pressure was gradually having an effect, and new planning applications were not effected unless the companies agreed to fill in the old holes with the quarry waste and replant the areas with trees. Attempts were also made to use the holes for the disposal of domestic and other waste, but these proposals foundered as no one could come up with a satisfactory method of sealing the areas, to prevent unknown harm being done to the water table which fed a large part of East Devon.

The Common

The Beacon in 1970, in its prime and showing its full compliment of trees.

Photo courtesy of the Express & Echo.

Woodbury Common has been the scene of many "events" over the Century, from use by the Military in the form of the Devon Yeomanry early on, being transformed into a replica of Exeter Airport during the last war so that German bombs fell there instead of on the proper one, and being a scene for a gangland murder in the 1970's.

In between all this it has always been an area of outstanding natural beauty and an area for recreation. No wonder that over the years various people have taken a stand for its preservation.

From the precincts of the ancient earthwork fortress, Woodbury Castle, and also the Beacon, some of the longest and best views in Devon can be enjoyed in good weather conditions. However, as with everything else, time takes its toll and the picture above does not reflect the current situation of the Beacon. The severe drought of 1976 left its mark on the raised mound, and many of the already nearly time-expired Scots Pines were brought to a premature end due solely to lack of water.

For many years following others also died, and gradually the whole area became very depleted. The problem was addressed by a co-operative effort between the Parish Council and the Clinton Devon Estates, who effected a replanting around the mound.

The replanting of trees surrounding the Beacon took place on 21st. April 1993.
Included in the picture on the right are:
The Hon. Mr. Charles Fane-Trefusis, son of the Landowner, Lord Clinton, Ursula Brighouse author of "Woodbury - A view from the Beacon", and Bungy Williams the Clinton Devon Estates Commons Warden.
The superb view from this point can be seen in the background.

THE LATER YEARS

This unique photograph below was taken by the Luftwaffe in 1942. Intelligence was obviously equally important then, as it is now. The picture depicts a large area of Woodbury Common, and clearly shows the dummy airfield that was cut out into the Common in the Castle-Four Firs-Yettington triangle to try to convince the German Air Force that this was Exeter airport.

Also in the picture the Dalditch Camp can be clearly seen, along with the Squabmoor reservoir, the Castle and Four Firs. Whilst a few bombs were dropped here, I think Gerry soon realised that there were no aircraft on the ground!

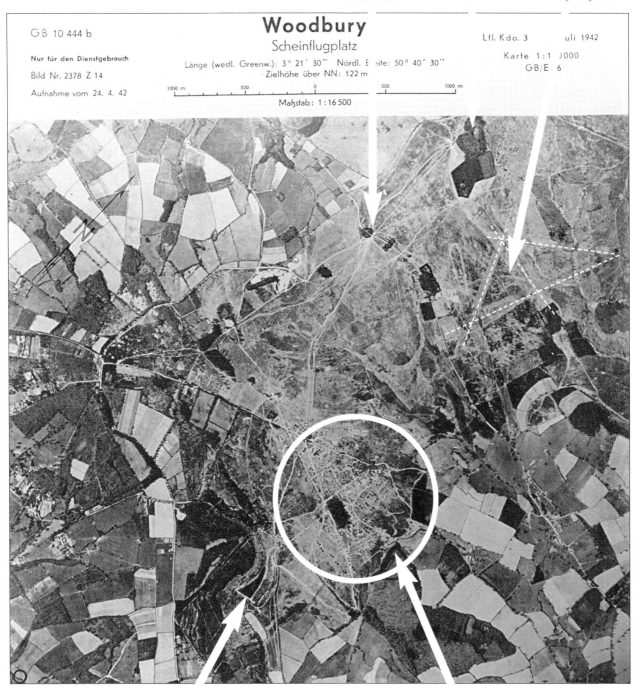

Four Firs   *The Castle*   *Dummy airfield*

Squabmoor reservoir   *Dalditch Camp*

TWENTIETH CENTURY WOODBURY

The Common being made up as it is of mainly combustible material, has always had a problem with fire. Sometimes it would be started accidentally by the military, sometimes by the sun shining on broken glass and unfortunately sometimes deliberately by persons unknown.

Whilst we only remember the events of our own lifetimes, the press reports fires on the Common right back to the early years of the century. Sadly of course most of these fires take place during the breeding season of the large compliment of bird life which inhabits the area. However, after all fires the Common seems to fight back with new growth. The saddest sight of all is to see the destruction of sometimes fifty-year-old plantations, which would normally be approaching their prime, and ready for harvesting.

The fire on the Common on the 14th. May 1984 was one of the most intense of the century.
Photo courtesy of the Express & Echo.

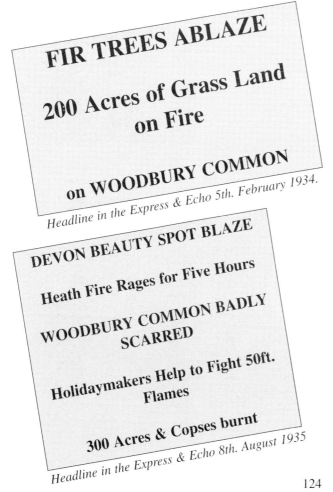

FIR TREES ABLAZE
200 Acres of Grass Land on Fire
on WOODBURY COMMON
Headline in the Express & Echo 5th. February 1934.

DEVON BEAUTY SPOT BLAZE
Heath Fire Rages for Five Hours
WOODBURY COMMON BADLY SCARRED
Holidaymakers Help to Fight 50ft. Flames
300 Acres & Copses burnt
Headline in the Express & Echo 8th. August 1935

FIRE ON WOODBURY COMMON
Water Pumped Two Miles from River Near Newton Poppleford

Ten thousand feet of hose were used by four brigades in an all night fight against a fierce heath fire detected last night on Woodbury Common, and even with their united efforts it took the brigades hours of hard work to completely subdue the flames. The firemen were assisted by members of the Devon County Police, including Sergt. Gould (Budleigh Salterton), Sergt. Taylor (Ottery St. Mary), Constable Rayner (Woodbury) and Sergt. Turner (Aylesbeare) together with a number of the Clinton Estate employees.

Second Officer Wain gave an Express & Echo representative some idea of the difficulties that had to be overcome. We were told that the nearest water supply was at Newton Poppleford some two miles away, but in the meantime another stream was found on the common side of Newton Poppleford. The men dammed up the stream and then the Exmouth pump lifted the water from the stream and pumped it to the Exeter engine. From there it was pumped to the Sidmouth engine, which in turn pumped it to the Ottery pump, which directed it onto the fire.

Express & Echo 1933.

The Doctors

Throughout my lifetime Woodbury has seen the passage of many doctors. It has also seen many different surgeries throughout the village.

My first recollection of the profession was to visit the surgery of Dr. Price at "The Grange" at the top of Broadway. Prior to him, I understand, Dr. Darbyshire practiced from "Thornleigh" in Town Lane and later from "The Gables" in Broadway. When Dr. Anthony Austin took over from Dr. Price in 1951 the surgery moved to "Claremont" in Mirey Lane.

When Dr. Austin married his assistant, the present Dr. Phyllis Austin, they required a larger premises and acquired "Springhayes" in Town Lane. Dr. Squires joined the practice whilst it was at "Springhayes", but due to Dr. Anthony Austin's severe decline in health, Dr. Phyl had to give up her position to nurse him.

Dr. Squires then left on his own with the assistance of his wife Daphne, moving the surgery to "temporary" premises in Town Lane. This is now long gone but can only be described as a tin shed, and was where No. 9 "Pollybrook" now stands.

Dr. Phyllis Austin.   Dr. Anthony Austin.

The picture above shows the old surgery which used to stand in Pollybrook. This "temporary" accommodation lasted for some 20 years!

Dr. Angela Douglas joined Dr. Squires as a partner in 1980, and of course is still with us. When Dr. Squires and his wife retired in 1988 Dr. Noel Lawn came in as a partner. As the years went on, the population of the village increased quite dramatically, and one of Dr. Squires' dreams was to be able to operate from a purpose built building large enough for the greater number of people he had to tend to.

After a lot of negotiating for a parcel of land on which to build such a premises, many of which were abortive, an area was secured on the present site within the new "Golden Heart" development. It was opened in 1986 two years before Dr. Squires retired, and has been sub-sequently extended.

This was the fulfilment of his vision and dream, and to him in particular Woodbury owes a debt of gratitude. Had it not been for his perseverance, we might all have had to go to Topsham every time we required attention.

Right:
Sheila Wright who was Dr. Squires' dispenser and "Woman Friday". She had the ability to answer the phone, dispense medicines, change dressings and answer the door all at the same time!

The medical team pictured outside the new surgery on the 6th. May 1986 when it opened. Dr. Squires is seen at the left, and his wife Daphne third left. Without her dedicated support he could not have managed.

125

Dr. Squires was a man with a tremendous sense of humour (which was probably a major asset in his job), and a great lover of the "Great Outdoors". There is no doubt that he should be classed as one of the century's "characters", a breed which is now sadly lacking! He would quite often be seen walking along Town Lane to the surgery swinging his stethoscope like a conker on a string, whistling at the same time. He jokingly said to me on several occasions that he was going to install a "Pill machine" outside the surgery suitably labelled, so that parishioners could put their money in and take the appropriate medicines, so that his workload could then be reduced! One of my main memories of the "Tin Shed" was that you always knew when you were "on". All you had to do was count up the number of people there when you arrived.... and wait! Nowadays it is slightly more difficult to arrive at the same answer, as there are up to three queues operating concurrently, but a waiting game is still the order of the day!

His most famous hour came in the winter snows of 1978, when the whole village was cut off totally for a week. He had been summoned to Yettington to attend a woman who was giving birth. I met him struggling on foot at Ford Water, and gave him a lift in the bucket of my tractor loader to Four Firs. Because of the drifts I could go no further, and he decided to walk on alone. I was not happy about his wellbeing, alone on the Common with no contact, in such conditions. I therefore returned about an hour later in a Land Rover to see if all was well. I found him stumbling back to Woodbury very cold and suffering from exposure, so he was duly bundled into the vehicle and taken home to warm up. From this episode his dedication to duty can only be seen as total. When he retired, the document below was drawn up to remind him of the affection and esteem that Woodbury residents held him in.

The Press said.... A Devon village turned out in force last night to say a remarkable farewell to its favourite doctor who was retiring after more than a quarter of a century in practice. In that time Dr. Guy Squires has dealt with more than 365,000 consultations in Woodbury and surrounding villages, and has become a friend to a huge rural community. More than 300 people packed into the village hall for an emotional retirement presentation, and many hundreds more contributed to a farewell cheque of £2829.29. A further tribute to the popular GP's many years of service will be paid later this week when the village church rings out a quarter peal on its bells. To mark the occasion, villager Hamish Palmer penned a poem, and Mary Cornick illustrated it with memorable scenes from the doctor's long career. Dr. Squires said that most of the time he had worked single handed, and it had been a hard slog, but he would not have swapped it for anything. He was now delivering children to children that he brought into the world when he first arrived as the village GP 26 years ago. There was hardly anyone he did not know by their christian name.

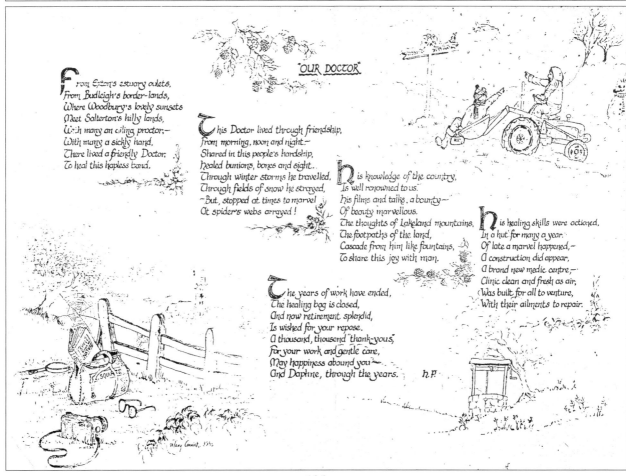

"OUR DOCTOR"

From Exton's estuary outlets,
From Budleigh's border-lands,
Where Woodbury's lovely sunsets
Meet Solterton's hilly lands,
With many an ailing proctor,—
With many a sickly hand,
There lived a friendly Doctor,
To heal this hapless band.

This Doctor lived through friendship,
from morning, noon and night:—
Shared in this people's hardship,
healed bunions, bones and sight..
Through winter storms he travelled,
Through fields of snow he strayed,
—But, stopped at times to marvel
At spider's webs arrayed !

his knowledge of the country,
Is well renowned to us:
his films and talks, a bounty—
Of beauty marvellous.
The thoughts of Lakeland mountains,
The footpaths of the land,
Cascade from him like fountains,
To share this joy with man.

his healing skills were actioned,
In a hut for many a year.
Of late a marvel happened,—
A construction did appear,
A brand new medic centre,—
Clinic clean and fresh as air,
Was built for all to venture,
With their ailments to repair.

The years of work have ended,
The healing bag is closed,
And now retirement splendid,
Is wished for your repose.
A thousand, thousand "thank-yous,
for your work and gentle care,
May happiness abound you—
And Daphne, through the years.   h.P.

Mary Cornick, 19??

The Church and Chapel

Both of these two institutions in the village of Woodbury have seen a few changes over the years. The Church of St. Swithun had its bells rehung onto a steel frame in the late 1950's, and had its tower exterior repointed and cleaned in 1994. The latter, which cost in the order of £150,000, was largely paid for by generous public subscription, and external grants.

The followers of the Free Church also had a major upheaval in the 1960's, when they moved from their long time base in the old Artillery Drill Hall in Broadway, to take over the rather dilapidated building of Christ Church. This had been built in 1851, but had remained unoccupied for several years. The move was brought about by a major increase in the Chapel following, which could no longer be accommodated at Broadway. However, much work had to be done to restore the new premises to a useful state, and expansion still continues in 1999 to meet the yet again increasing demand.

Left:
Many hands make light work of manoeuvring the bells out of the Church tower in 1959.

Below:
The shrouded tower in 1994, which remained in this guise for the best part of a year, so that cleaning and repointing could take place in all weathers.

Above:
The bells which had been sent to the Whitechapel Bell Foundry in London, had now returned having been retuned. Their new shiny insides can be seen.

In the picture are left to right back row:
HJ Briggs, A (Tony) Gooding, Jim Gooding, Harry Miller, Victor Fox, Ken Dawe, John Glanvill (senr.), John Glanvill (junr.).
Front row: Jack Sellick, Rev. Alec Osmond, AG Betts, C. Morrish, Alfie Stamp, Bertie Stamp and WJ (Bill) Reeves and Harry Stokes Churchwardens. On the right Bill Theobald, a fitter from the Whitechapel Bell Foundry.

TWENTIETH CENTURY WOODBURY

When Christ Church was taken over the ancient burial ground was overgrown and the remaining tombstones leaning at all angles. These were later removed to the perimeter of the area.
The bell turret similar to the one on the School was in poor condition and had to be taken down.

Picture left:
Inside the old building time had taken its toll, and Mrs Harold Ware is seen looking over the upper storey, which had to be removed, although in 1999 there was a move to reinstate it.

Picture right:
Christ Church has always been a champion of Woodbury children's religious education at weekly Sunday Schools, and later to youth clubs for the older ones. The extension seen in the picture was added to assist in this purpose, providing kitchen facilities as well.
It is now a thriving Church and still bursting at the seams.

The Schools

Throughout the later years of the century both schools have undergone much improvement and change, in both the fabric and the methods of teaching. This can only be to the benefit of the pupils. When I was at the school in the 1940's, things were very different, and all the buildings were pretty basic by today's standards.

During the 60's an extension was added to Woodbury School to give extra and better classrooms, followed by the installation of a swimming pool. This required much fund raising by the PTA and others. When I was there the playground was much smaller at the back, and terminated with a popple wall across roughly where the gate now is into the playground. There was no grass field for sports. This was purchased later when the house at the top, previously called "Yonderhaye" (to which it belonged), was sold and added to the school facilities. Computers were installed in the 1980's, and now even small children are computer literate. Of course this is an essential requirement of the time we now live in.

Left: A class c.1960, featuring some well-known faces, and showing the popple wall mentioned above.

*Above:
A class c.1970.*

*Above:
The new swimming pool was opened in June 1961, by Mr Philip, the Chief Education Officer.*

*Above:
Terence Marks, ?, Frank Smith, Rodney Ford.*

TWENTIETH CENTURY WOODBURY

During 1971, the school celebrated its centenary, and in May of that year held a centenary fete. No fete is complete without its Queen, and this year was to be no exception.

The unique picture at the bottom of the page shows the School 100 years before, in its last stages of completion in October 1871, when it was opened. Men can be seen still working on the scaffolding around the entrance porch, and the access to Town Lane is somewhat narrower than today.

Mr Harry Stokes crowning the May Queen Sharon Temple. Her attendants were Sandra Doran, Susan Bazely, Nicola Blazer, Clare Vanstone and Alison Seymour.

Dancing in the playground to celebrate the School's Centenary.

PHOTOGRAPHED BY. J.F.LONG. 45, HIGH ST EXETER.

R. MEDLEY FULFORD. ARCHT. THE CLOSE, EXETER.

THE NEW SCHOOL, WOODBURY, OPENED OCTR 18TH 1871.

THE LATER YEARS

Salterton School has always been a thriving establishment, and been very "go-ahead". Whilst a lot smaller in size than Woodbury itself, it was its smallness that attracted British Telecom to take a look at it in 1987. It was chosen as the smallest school in the country to be set up for an experimental e-mail link with a school in Tasmania.

Just outside the school entrance there once stood what was called in Salterton "The Great Tree". This was reputed to be 200 years old. On the 25th. January 1990 the British Isles was hit by storms of monumental proportions, and the said tree was to become a victim, ending it's long life like so many others in our area. It was a sad day indeed for the village as a whole.

The e-mail experiment was the beginning of technology which led to the Internet. Salterton School was therefore at the cutting edge of a new era. This picture was sent to every BT subscriber in the country.

"The Great Tree" before and after the storms of 25th. January 1990.

Woodbury Salterton School 1979.
*Christian names only are available. They are **from back left to right:***
Joanne, Chantal, Daniel, Nick, Vicky, Daryl, Rebecca, David,

Julia, Troy, Damion, Susan, Eric, Tina, Julie, Linda, Mark, Helen,

Andrea, Britt, Kay, F. Burrell, G. Dearnley, H. Pyatt, Nicola, Pratt, Gary,

Paula, Donna, Naomi, Michelle, Philip, Nicola, Martin, Sarah.

The Cider Makers

During the whole of the Century cider making has taken place in the Parish. In the early years most farms would have had their own equipment to process the apples from their own, and the many other orchards in the area. Cider was an important part of the staple diet of all good farm workers. Whereas we may take a cup of coffee or tea when we take a break during the day, they would resort to the cider bottle for comfort. As their jobs then were almost 100% physical compared with today, perhaps they also got their strength from the apple.

Rural cider making waned during the 1950's as the larger cider makers took over and orchards were scrubbed out, but the art has never completely died out in our parish. Made in Woodbury "Scrumpy" as it is known can still be obtained if you know where to go!

For many years in the recent past cider was made annually at Gillbrook, where an old press still remains. When this ceased, Norman Bowles of Woodmanton Farm decided to renovate his old and disused press, and bring it back into production. Five local lads, assisted by Norman's expertise in the matter, enjoyed many years of production at Woodmanton until he retired in 1980. Luckily they took a lot of photographs, so the method is not lost. Since then limited production has continued from Woodbury's last remaining working press.

The cider making process requires much effort. First of all the apples have to be picked up from the orchard floor.

Robin Chapman is seen taking the sacks of apples into the loft, from where they were put through the apple mill.

Coming down through the mill they fall into a large container, in this case the bottom half of a barrel.

All the collected material is then placed on the press and covered with straw to make a "cheese". This has to be neatly trimmed with a hay knife, to keep it tidy.

The juice is collected in the other half of the barrel.

At this point, the power of the press is brought to bear on the "Cheese". This requires considerable effort, and needs constant tightening up to make the juice flow.

Constant sampling is a definite requirement of the process, to check clarity and taste!

As in all good things, the final product had to undergo rigorous testing, and the experts from the local "authority" are brought in to make sure that the end product gets its seal of approval!

So the art of cider making is passed down to another generation, as has been the practice over the years. Pictured are Gary Radford, Kevin Hawkins, Dave Olesky and Chris Biddulph.

In another quarter, Trixie and Brian Sellick assisted by Nigel Smeath are turning on the pressure at the Gillbrook press in the 1970's. It is understood that two hogsheads of this brew found their way to a well known pub in Exmouth weekly, on the coal merchant's empty lorry!

Woodmanton Farm

The area known as Woodmanton is just to the south-east of Woodbury village, and was until recently a purely agricultural area. There were four farmsteads within a distance of half a mile of each other, making a tight knit community. Mostly Rolle Estate (now Clinton Devon Estates) farms they had all been tenanted by at least one generation of the same family, but in some cases more. It was traditional earlier in the century for sons to follow fathers in the tenancy, but this is no longer the case, for various reasons.

Farms usually changed tenants on the retirement of "father", but in some cases there might be no one to follow on. During the period from 1970 to the present day, many farms were amalgamated to make them more viable units to compete in the modern world. Such a case came about at Woodmanton Farm where Norman Bowles came to retirement age at a point in time where it would not have been economic for an incoming tenant to take it on. The buildings, like so many in the parish were built around the 1880's, when the Rolle Estate carried out a major farm building programme. They were built for the horse and cart, and modern machinery became so large that it could not enter most of them. The cost to rebuild them to the standard required would have been prohibitive, therefore other uses were sourced. No, not for cider making, but for more industrial enterprises- the making of teapots!

It is always a sad day when a farmer has to see his assets auctioned off, after a lifetime of hard work by all members of the family. Much harder than the average person could ever realise. During the 1980's however this day came for the Bowles family.

The end of the line at Woodmanton farm, when the cattle are sold in a makeshift ring, surrounded by local farmers and buyers, and by purely casual observers.

Mr. Bowles was leaving the farm after 64 years, having arrived there when he was just two years old with his father and mother!

He later married another Woodbury farmer's daughter, Patricia Glanvill, so the farming commitment was total. Throughout his lifetime he has been an active participant in many village affairs and you will have seen many pictures in this book in which he is featured. Far from his image of being the joker in the village carnivals or prospective mayor, he was a founder member of the Woodbury Young Farmers Club, a Parish Councillor for around 40 years, a special constable for 30 years and a school manager for many years.

At the sale above, the family peacock realised £32, and the top price of £625 was fetched for store cattle. Some difference from his father's time!

THE LATER YEARS

The farmyard is seen here in the days after the sale.

Everything was left clean, and the old building on the right which had housed the cider press would no longer echo with the the sounds and smells of cider making.

The fine old building of the granary stands in the background.

The front garden gate and wall at Woodmanton is typical of the Rolle Estate design of the time.

The popple and flint walling is repeated on many a farm in this area, as is the rather large squarish design of the farm house itself.

All was built to last, which it is doing very well.

The old wagon shed was situated across the road from the main farmstead.

It clearly shows the lowness which was not suitable for later century tractors and machinery.

The Village Hall

By 1980 the Village Hall was in need of a major refit. It had been in operation since 1910 when it had been bought as a redundant chapel in Topsham, and re-erected in the village. Little had been done to it since then except for the addition of a porch and the small room. Since the 1960's in particular, the population of the village was increasing at quite a fast rate and the hall was becoming quite inadequate to host large gatherings. It had always been long and narrow, which was not at all ideal for dances, as with a row of chairs along each side there was not sufficient room to "let yourself go" in some of the more energetic ballroom dances.

After a great deal of fund raising within the village, backed up by grants and interest free loans from the local authority, and members of the public, work went ahead to put a steel frame over the top of the existing building. This made the building wider on the lower side, therefore making it a lot better for a host of things. The whole operation was conducted within a very small space surrounding the hall, which did not make it easy for any mechanisation. Once the new roof was put on the steel frame, the old one was taken off from beneath, keeping the whole operation in the dry. A new kitchen and toilet was added, and the hall came back into service with great acclaim.

Left:
The wall was demolished to gain access, but subsequently rebuilt to match. The hall's original corrugated iron structure can be clearly seen.

Below left:
The steel frame is put over the top of the existing building.

Below:
A giant crane had to be used because of the long reach involved.

THE LATER YEARS

In 1981 a new floor was laid on the old joists, and by 1997 it became apparent that there was a dampness problem which was causing the joists to rot. The hall therefore went through another refit and expansion in 1998. A new floor was laid with major works in the form of sub walls to support it. The stage and changing rooms were rebuilt to great advantage. With the co-operation of the Royal British Legion, monies that they had available for a club building (a project which had never materialised) were also spent to improve the rear quarter of the building into office space for the parish council. This area had been left as a void in the 1981 project. Currently we have a good hall which is well used by all.

Left:
As with the 1981 refit restricted access made the job equally difficult. A hole was made in one end through which the debris was removed.

Right:
In the confined space the contractors used a mini digger and small dumper truck to excavate and remove the soil for the sub walls' foundations.

Left:
The sub walls were finally erected and the new floor, with new joists, constructed on the top.

The "Woodbury News"

Since the early 1960's, as has been previously mentioned, the population of the parish was expanding at a fast rate. Instead of it being still a close knit community, people were moving in to the new properties from "outside". These people sometimes had different ideas to the "locals", and in a few cases some resentment used to build up.

As it was difficult to dispense news of what was happening within the parish, and to try to resolve some of the occurring differences between the various factions,

Mrs Ursula Brighouse and a band of enthusiastic followers started a local magazine in 1964. This was called the "Woodbury News", and it has been going ever since. At the time it was one of the first such village publications to be produced, since followed by many other villages. Over the years it has proved a very useful medium, but is run on a shoestring budget so that it can be affordable by all. During its 36 year life so far, it has only had two editors, the first Mrs Brighouse, followed latterly by Dr. David Keep.

The normal monthly edition of the Woodbury News has a pictorial cover depicting a local historical house or scene, usually drawn by a local resident. Latterly old photographs have been used at times to illustrate the "goings on" from days gone by.

Usually every two years in January, a directory of all things available in the parish is printed. This ranges from Local Government, Medical Services, the Churches, Public Transport, Shops and Services and a listing of all clubs and societies. This takes a lot of work to compile, but is a major asset to any newcomer to the area.

Later Century People

The lives of many of the people in this section of the book will have spanned two thirds of the century, and their names may have cropped up before. If they have it is because they have probably been at the forefront of village and parish life through-out much of their time. Some are sadly no longer with us, but many of us hold fond memories of good friendships and happy times with these people. They still are, or were, the salt of the earth.

*James (Jim) Briggs
who ran the Post Office.*

*His wife Winnie, daughter of William Daley
who built the new Post Office in 1912.*

*Mr Dearnley, long time headmaster of
Salterton school seen here leaving on his
retirement.*

*Jack (Keeper) Pavey and his wife on the occasion of their
diamond wedding anniversary*

Henry Sage from Salterton, a master with a Devon shovel. His thoughts do not need any text! **Photo courtesy the Express & Echo.**

Centre: *Reggie Bishop, a master craftsman in the carpentry trade, seen here with a trap he had restored from Bridge Farm. He is flanked by the two George Wilsons, old George and young George. Reggie's apprenticeship in earlier times qualified him as a wheelwright, amongst other things, so he was capable of (a) making a cartwheel and (b) fitting an iron tyre to it. He once made a set of stairs for myself, after taking only three measurements, height, width and depth. A pencil was taken from behind his ear and the information was transferred to a cigarette packet! On arrival, the stairs fitted perfectly without any adjustment.*

Trixie Sellick when he was the postman. Prior to this he spent many years in farm work.

Trixie's wife Joan at the pump at Haydons Cottage. Until the mid 80's this was her only water supply. You always knew when she was coming because she had an infectious laugh which preceeded her!

THE LATER YEARS

During the 1940's Bill Summerfield was the top Woodbury gardener, winning all the prizes at the village flower shows. During the later years of the century, this mantle was taken on by Bob Miller. His plot opposite Phoenix Motors can only be described as the ultimate vegetable garden. The immaculate rows have been photographed by many a visitor to Woodbury, and the area is indeed a credit to him.

He has won so many prizes that they are too numerous to document here, but his crowning glory came in 1987 when he was awarded a certificate from the Guinness Book of Records for growing the largest recorded shallots. It is understood that this record has never been broken. These can be seen in the picture beside and compared with those of usual size.

Above:
Bob Miller in 1987.

Certificate

GUINNESS BOOK OF RECORDS

R MILLER

LARGEST SHALLOT

5 lb 13 oz 2.636 kg

WOODBURY, EXETER, DEVON

1987

NORRIS McWHIRTER

Right:
The immaculate layout of a perfect weed free garden.

Woodbury has always had a flow of talented people. Pippa Thompson is no exception. When the book to celebrate the Parish Council Centenary was published in 1994, Pippa used her artistic skills to design and paint an illustrated parish map. This was printed to accompany the book, and is still available, as a reprint was commissioned in 1998.

Pippa is seen on the left at work on the map.

Right: *Sarah and Percy Sharland. Sadly no longer with us, they both led interesting lives. In her early days, Sarah spent much of her time "In service" in some of the area's upper class houses, and married Percy at Woodbury Salterton church in 1925, after four years of good old fashioned courting. Percy was then working for Henry Sage at Bridge Farm as horseman.*

He then came to work for my father at Webbers Farm, where he stayed for 25 years. He was awarded the "Order of Industrial Heroism" in 1960, after an incident with a bull. When taken to hospital he was given two anaesthetics, neither of which put him to sleep so that his broken arm could be mended! Other methods had to be resorted to. In retirement his passion was collecting miniature bottles, seen on the right.

Sid Baker and his wife Winnie are seen on the left. They celebrated their Golden wedding in 1978. Both born locally they married at Aylesbeare Church in 1928 after which they lived at School Cottages in Woodbury Salterton.
Sid joined the Devonshire Regiment in 1914, and was twice wounded at Hill 60 and the Battle of the Somme. He returned as a volunteer farm worker until the end of the War at Colebrook near Crediton, before moving back to Salterton where apart from a brief spell of farm work, joined Devon County Council as a roadman for a further 27 years.
Before she was married Mrs Baker was Miss Preston from Aylesbeare.
Sadly they are no longer with us.

Woodbury's oldest resident

Above:

Mrs Nancy Hollett, aged 100 years and 8 months when this photograph was taken on Midsummer's Day 1999. Since then she has attained her 101st. birthday. Born on the 6th. October 1898 in the Tiverton area, she went to London to work during the First World War at Bourne & Hollingsworth's department store. During her time off she would help to nurse casualties of the bombing. Two years later she returned to Devon, residing in the Teignmouth area, where she also took wounded soldiers out in bath chairs. At that time she used to frequent the "Seven Stars" pub at Kennford, where she met her husband to be. "It was either him or the son of the Seven Stars", she recalls! Some time was spent manning a shop in Barnstaple, but she and her husband took over "The Firs" in Bonds Lane in the 1930's. From there they ran a farm with a milk round around the village. "It was hard work", she says, although it certainly does not seem to have done her any harm! She is the only person in Woodbury who has lived through the whole of the period of this century.

Maybe shortly, she will be able to say that she has lived in three centuries.

Picture left:

Mrs Evelyn Leach follows fairly closely behind. She was born in 1911, and is the daughter of Frank Turner, who was featured earlier in the book preparing to go to military camp on George Wilson's horse in 1900.

She too now lives in Bonds Lane but began her life at Yates Cottages.

She went to Salterton School at the age of three, and when her father's employment moved to Postlake Farm, she had to walk daily to school from there. "People used to work in those days", she recalls, "and they thrived on it". A remarkable woman, who can tell many a tale, some of which are recalled in Sally and Ramsay Elliot's book.

TWENTIETH CENTURY WOODBURY

Many village people have given more than half a lifetime to the pursuit of village affairs, be it parish council, district council or just purely getting things done. Most have had little thanks for the work that they have put in over the years, but without these people's contributions the parish would be a poorer place. Many have already been pictured in the book, alongside what they were doing, but others have had little recognition. A few of them whose photographs are available are seen here.

Gordon Hallett.
Parish Councillor from 1952 - 1999.
Also many years a District Councillor.

Harry Stokes
Parish Councillor 1943 - 1984.
Also many years a District Councillor.

Lewis Brown
Parish Councillor for a short period, but the best Father Christmas that any Woodbury children's party has ever had. His annual appearance was in great demand!

Margaret Smith
Parish Councillor 1970 - 1999 and postwoman for many years.

Jim Gooding, left, *seen handing over the keys on his retirement as caretaker of the Village Hall for 40 years and **Valentine DuBuisson, right,** without whose determination and drive neither the new Village Hall or the new cricket ground would have become a reality.*

Cricketing

The cricket club has been an ongoing organisation for a long period of time. From about 1948 to 1968 its grounds were in a section of the field above "Oakhayes". At that time it was a strong club and had a lot of support. A pavilion was erected at the grand cost of £87.5s., which was constructed of rough hewn elm lap boards. Wives of the cricketers would attend matches to provide the teams with teas, and it was a generally sociable occasion. Sports and other events also took place in this field, which in the 1930's had been used for the village flowershow and gymkhana.

Eventually, as in most organisations, the numbers of those willing to help with the upkeep of the grounds, and the general running of the club dwindled away, and the club as such went into "hibernation" for several years.

A new generation then came on to the scene, with a renewed vigor. For many years they played at Clyst St. George, as their home ground, but by the 1990's great pressure was applied to the Parish Council for a ground of their own. This eventually materialised in a field in Town Lane, probably the wettest field in Woodbury, but with the availability of Sports Council and other grants and loans, the field was drained, bulldozed level, seeded and now forms probably one of the best village cricket pitches in the area, with its outstanding location and fine views over a vast distance. Its pavilion however, which was built voluntarily largely by Ken Sellick and helpers, cost rather more than the original at c. £30,000.00!

Left:
The pavilion and old nissen hut in the former cricket field in Oakhayes Road. Bob Miller (senr.) who was chief groundsman at the time, is seen sitting on the mower.

Right:
Seen here are left to right back row:
Leonard Hallett, Lionel Goss, Jack ?, ?, Derek Channon.
Front row: Bob Fox, Bert Skinner, Bob Miller, Roy Summerfield, Stan Gooding, Doug Hammond.
c.1960

Left and below:
The new cricket field and pavilion, (not quite completed), with the first match in progress the 3rd. July 1994.

Twinning

The dawn of a new era, which was spawned by the creation of the European Union, brought with it a desire to get better acquainted with our continental neighbours.

Devon in particular was a leader in this process, and at that time Devon County Council appointed a twinning officer for Devon called Frank Claxton. He was instrumental in the setting up of a contact between Woodbury and Bretteville-sur-Odon in Brittany. Several exploratory visits took place by a newly formed twinning committee, to make sure we were compatible, prior to the signing of the Charter on Easter Saturday 25th. March 1978 on the village green, with due pomp and ceremony. On 22nd. October of the same year a reciprocal Charter was signed in Bretteville, followed by a champagne reception in the Mairie. We subsequently named a road "Bretteville Close", and the French named one of their roads "Avenue de Woodbury". Since then the twinning association has flourished with many visits both ways.

Left:
Signing the Charter on the Green. From left to right are: Roger Stokes, Mme. Yvette Monier, the French deputy mayor, Frank Claxton, Ted Neather, Eric Ware, (Chairman of Woodbury Parish Council), and Mme. Audoli, (Chairwoman of the Bretteville committee).

Right:
Following the ceremony a wreath was placed on the War Memorial, by the representatives of both communities.

Left:
Later in the year in Bretteville, the second part of the Charter was signed by Mayor Vasseur on behalf of the French, and by Eric Ware on our behalf.
Seen also in the picture are left, Tony Palmer, and second left Hamish Palmer (no relation), who were both major mainstays of the organisation at that time.

Any other business!

Some things in the course of history can be classed more as one off events, and have no long term story. Nevertheless these events need to be documented, as they are factual events which have taken place.

The pages that follow will show some of the other things that have happened in the parish since 1960. Some have had their share of controversy, and some have been consilitory in their happening.

"The Berlin Wall"

In the early 1980's when the so called "Golden Heart" was built, there was much friction regarding points of pedestrian access to the main village road. It was thought that "newcomers" would integrate better with the locals if the new residents could mix whilst walking down the main street. Hence several access points were detailed. However this was not to some locals liking, and one night a group of individuals built a block wall topped by barbed wire across the proposed access to the Green. This became known as "The Berlin Wall", and despite council efforts to remove it, it still remains today!

"The Annual Bonfire"

In 1986 there had been moves to remove the annual bonfire from the Green, it's hereditary spot for centuries. This caused some stir in the village, and this group of ladies were seen to be guarding it with their life.

"Parking problems"

Around 1970, the village had a brand new car park constructed beside the village hall at a cost of £6000.
However, press reports said that few people were using it, as it was too far from the centre, and that children were using it more as a playground. Meanwhile, the Green had remained an impromptu parking area, not approved of by some.
All photos courtesy of the Express & Echo.

TWENTIETH CENTURY WOODBURY

In the late 1980's the villagers of Woodbury Salterton formed a link with the village of Dumbutu in The Gambia. Seventy five percent of Salterton households took part in this exercise, with the criteria to foster community relationships, and provide assistance to Dumbutu which would help make the villagers there self sufficient. This proved a great success, and exchange visits took place. Seen here on a Gambian visit to Salterton in 1994 are Gambians Kawsa Demba, Essa Drammeh and Nyima Darbo, with residents John and Margaret Pickering, Dr. Hugh and Mrs Powell, Liz Appleton and Christine Bricknell.

Stallcombe House, a residential unit for mentally handicapped persons, was set up in the late 1970's. Situated in Sanctuary Lane it used the house and buildings of the old farm as a base. Over the years much improvement has taken place here, along with an organic farm.
1993 saw the opening of the Stallcombe House residential extension, pictured here, with Alan Wright the Principal and his wife Maureen.

Before it was cleaned and re-pointed in 1994, it was noticed that a certain amount of vegetation was growing from various ledges on the tower of St. Swithuns Church.
Unsure how to tackle the problem the Church authorities enlisted the help of the Royal Marines.
What better than a bit of abseiling practice, and Sgt. Dave Ford is seen here showing that it was all in a day's work!

All photos courtesy of the Express & Echo

In February 1993, the future of the red phone box was under threat. It had been proposed to replace it with a new modern style one.
At the time there was an attempt to get it listed, which was not successful, Cyril Rowsell who runs the hardware store opposite volunteered to keep an eye on it during daylight hours, and British Telecom decided to leave it in situ.

The centuries old art of thatching still regularly takes place in the parish. There are still a large number of properties that support a thatched roof. The average life of such a roof is 25 - 30 years. Tom Radford's cottage opposite the Green is seen being re-thatched in 1970. It has subsequently been done again in 1998. Idyllic it may be, but expensive it certainly is! A newly thatched roof however is a work of art.

In the 1990's as people were beginning to become more environmentally conscious, and more information seemed to be required by all as a matter of course, the Clinton Devon Estates erected these superb Devon Pebblebed Heath boards at Woodbury Castle, which showed the flora and fauna and bird life that existed in the area.
Lord Clinton is seen here with Frank Lock, the Chairman of East Devon District Council in 1992, at the unveiling ceremony.
All photos courtesy of the Express & Echo.

Left:
Over the years the parish has had its share of extreme weather. The picture here shows the "Diggers Rest" at Salterton with a covering of snow for Christmas 1962.
Photo courtesy the Express & Echo.

Right:
Whilst winter snow does not seem so prevelant at the end of the century, 1978 brought the most severe fall since 1947.
At the top of Globe Hill seen here, the snow completely filled the road between the hedges, making it impassable for days.

Left:
During the 1978 winter the whole village was cut off from the outside world by two metre high drifts, which were difficult to clear because of the narrow lanes.
Cyril Clarke, the milkman, is seen here delivering milk in Longpark by milk churn and sled. The milk had come from Webbers Farm, who could not get a tanker in to take it away. Everyone survived the encounter, and had a few amusing stories to tell afterwards!

Left:
1994 saw the centenary of the Parish Council. The picture shows those in office at that time. **From left to right back row they are:** *Clerk Alex Sanders, Geoff Stevens, Gordon Hallett, Nick Sanders, Philip Glanvill, Ivor Loman, Oliver Robinson.* **Front row:** *Margaret Smith, Ada Follett, John Adams (Chairman), Jane Logan and Dr. Phyllis Austin.*

Right:
The celebrations were marked in particular by the holding of a street party on the Arch. The road was closed and tables neatly laid for the childrens party.

Left:
The occasion required a "Princess" who was crowned at the Village Hall. She was Lisa White, aged 8, centre, seen here with her attendants sister Emily, aged 7, and Lizzie Sanders aged 5.

Right:
The party covered the whole area of the Arch, and was a memorable occasion for the children in particular.

No change!

As we come to the end of the 20th. Century, another hundred years of life in Woodbury parish, it is interesting to note that in many respects little has changed at all. Despite all the progress from the horse and cart as the main form of transport, to now being able to travel faster than the speed of sound in an aeroplane, and send your mail down the telephone line to arrive the other end almost before it has left your desk, much of Woodbury remains virtually as it was in 1900.

Of course there are more houses, and a larger population, but this is no different to any other community.

Most of the cob built houses of the 19th. Century are still intact in our parish, and in the last 40 years many of these have been re-furbished by their owners to keep them going into the 21st. Century. Previously these would have been demolished as they became the worse for wear. A few pictures follow which show a "then and now" view of various village aspects which are largely similar.

1910 - 1999

All Change!

Top above:
Webbers Farm in the 1940's and 1960's with cattle.
Lower above:
Converted for human habitation in 1984.

Above:
*The Beeches early in the century, when in its former glory.
It had its own grass tennis court, and no wire netting was
allowed around it. Players plus a spaniel used to find lost balls!*
Right:
*In 1999, the house can be seen on the left of the picture, but the
grass court has been replaced by a housing estate and road.*

TWENTIETH CENTURY WOODBURY

Whilst on the previous page I have indicated that much of the fabric of the parish has changed little, on the other side of the fence, that of income earning, there have been considerable changes from the early part of the century. Agriculture, which used to be the main employer in the rural areas, is certainly no longer in the same position. Years of modernisation and efficiency have ultimately taken their toll. It has now become too efficient, and can produce too much food too easily with less labour.

Food therefore has become so cheap that the farmers who produce it can no longer make a reasonable living from agriculture alone. In the 1970's and 80's a new word appeared - "diversification". The government encouraged farmers to look at other ways of making a living, whilst still tending the land. Shops also had to diversify to survive, as did other businesses. The advent of large supermarkets has put considerable pressure on rural shops. For everyday needs, Woodbury parish now only has two remaining shops compared with all those listed on pages 69 - 72 in earlier years. Should it come to pass that these become extinct, the parish may no longer remain a community, with a community spirit, but it could well become just another mundane place on a map.

Left:
Due to the effects of diversification in the parish, changes have occurred here. Fields that were previously occupied by creatures of the four legged variety, are now being occupied by those with two! Tourism in its many different forms can be seen in many areas. By and large most tourism businesses have a vested interest in keeping the area looking at its best for the visitor. The visitor in his turn provides income for the local area, which helps keep the village shops going during this uncertain period of time.

Below:
There are now very few farmhouses in the parish which do not offer visitor accommodation of an extremely high standard, like Cottles Farm. In the early years of the century such an operation would have been unheard of.

Above right:
Local industry has also had to diversify. Blackhill Quarry has always had an engineering division. Normally making quarrying equipment, they have branched out, and the picture shows an oil head desander destined for Oman, which was built in Woodbury in 1998. They have exported to China, India, Canada and the South Atlantic.

Of course, we are not the only ones to have passed this way!

Because of its long and torturous history, going well back into the Bronze Age, and the site of a Roman earthwork fortress within its midst, Woodbury has always been a place of interest to those of an enquiring nature.

In 1933, a Mr GEL Carter carried out major excavations on Woodbury Common in the area of the Castle. After a lot of digging by hand on various burial mounds between the Castle and Blackhill House, he considered he had found evidence of heathen worship on the Common. The press of the time reveals that he found a bird outline in blue stones, and various lines of blue stones pointing in specific directions. The blue bird is held to show association with the early Aryian religion of Asia, so we must have been on the map even in those early days.

Nowadays it is easier to find memorabilia that has "been left behind". Today's tool is the metal detector, which if used properly disturbs little but finds a lot. Three local people, Nigel Tucker and Gerald and Pauline Miles, have over the last few years been carrying out a systematic scanning of the surrounding area. Meticulously recorded, they show that an interesting lot of people have trodden Woodbury soil. Some of their finds are listed below.

Bridle boss or rosette.
Late 18th - 19th. Century.

John Penny 1204 -1209 Short cross.
Changed to long cross in 1247 to prevent clipping.

Elizabeth I sixpence 1573.
Third issue.

Henry VI Groat 1424 - 1427.
Annulet issue from the Calais Mint.

Centenionalis of Flavius Magnentius AD 350 - 353.
Made of copper - minted in Lyons AD 352.

Victorian Copper Alloy filigree button.

The above included by kind permission of Nigel Tucker.

*A Globe Hotel Woodbury token,
which was used as a form of currency
early in the century.*

*A shoulder plate of the Armed Association which
was formed in 1798. Their prime objective was to
provide a home defence against invasion.*

*A decorative cast bronze pouring spout from
the 15th. or 16th. century.*

*A post medieval sword pommel with flat
topped knob, dating from the 17th. century.*

*16th. century snake belt fasteners. These were used as
part of a sword belt in place of the normal buckle.
They fell out of fashion in the 17th. century, but came
back in the 18th.*

*Late 17th. century foot patten. These were fixed
under the shoes of the ladies to give them extra
height to keep their long skirts out of the mud.*

The above included by kind permission of Gerald and Pauline Miles.

A Bronze Age axehead found by the author whilst following a plough at Rushmore Farm below Woodbury Castle in 1960. Three thousand years old, it was as sharp as the day it was dropped!

And finally...

I hope that after reading this book you will have been given an insight into some of the events, or had some memories refreshed as to what life was really like during the century. However, as the 20th. Century draws to a close one mystery still remains....

Who burnt the Headmaster's canes?

The answer to this closely guarded secret has never been divulged. This event took place in the 1930's at Woodbury school. The then headmaster Mr Kinsman, was well known for his liberal use of the cane on a daily basis for any minor misdemeanour. Eventually a small group of the young pupils decided that they had had enough of such treatment, and decided to do something about it One morning during assembly, they sneaked out and took six canes out of the headmaster's cane rack. These one of them put into the school boiler, never to be seen again! Repercussions were harsh indeed, but those responsible swore a pact of secrecy that they would never divulge who actually put them in the boiler. That pact is still in force 70 years later, and neither of the two surviving members of that group will let on as to "Who dunnit!"

I also have been sworn to secrecy, and asked not to name them, so I have hidden their pictures behind this text. The mystery therefore remains intact!

However, I have got my own ideas!

LIST OF SUBSCRIBERS

Mr John D. Adams, Woodbury, Devon

Mrs D. Alford, Exton, Exeter, Devon

Diane Alford, Exton, Exeter, Devon

Jeanette Appleby, Brislington, Bristol

Valerie Arndt, Woodbury, Devon

Mr David L. Asprey, Exmouth, Devon

Mr & Mrs R. Astle, Clevedon, Somerset

Dr Phyllis Austin, Woodbury, Devon

Albert E. Bale, Cardiff, Wales

Edwin Bamsey, Woodbury Salterton, Devon

Mrs M. Barriball, Woodbury, Devon

Brenda Bennett (née Wilson), Westleigh, Tiverton, Devon

Mr P. Bertram, Exmouth, Devon

Joyce Biddulph, Woodbury, Devon

Mary Birchmore, Exton, Exeter, Devon

Mrs E. M. Birks, Woodbury Salterton, Devon

Marjorie E. M. Bishop, Exton, Devon

Julia M. L. Bond, Exmouth, Devon

Mrs R. Bowden, Woodbury, Devon

Peter James Briggs, Woodbury, Devon

Dr Martin W. Briggs, Broadstone, Dorset

Ursula (Bunty) Brighouse, Woodbury, Devon

Mrs Jenny Broom (née Wakley), Clyst-St-George, Devon

Reg Brown, Woodbury, Devon

Mrs Dora Brown, Woodbury, Devon

Raymond & Mary Brown, Woodbury, Devon

Mrs H. Brown, Cullompton, Devon

Alan & Linda Brown, Exmouth, Devon

K. J. Burrow, Bucks Cross, Bideford, Devon

The Capewell Family, Woodbury, Devon

Mr S. Charles-Davis, Colaton Raleigh, Devon

Liz, Dave & Thomas Cherrett, Woodbury Salterton, Devon

Den & Teresa Clark, Hedge End, Southampton

Don Clemens, Woodbury, Devon

David & Dina Clement, Exton, Exeter, Devon

L. John Clotworthy, Crewkerne, Somerset

Judith & John Coker, Somersall, Chesterfield, Derby

Michelle Conneeley, Woodbury, Devon

Mrs E. G. Cooke, Woodbury, Devon

Jeffrey Dagworthy, Woodbury Salterton, Devon

John Daley, Poole, Dorset

John & Pauline Danzelman, Exmouth, Devon

Shirley Ann, Sophia Mary & Laura Ellen Dart, Woodbury, Devon

Mr M. J. Davieson, Woodbury Salterton, Exeter, Devon

David F. Deacon, Woodbury, Devon

Roger & Liz Dinnis, Woodbury, Devon

Paul & Angela Douglas, Woodbury, Devon

Roma Downs, Woodbury Salterton, Devon

Geoffrey & Rosemary Downs (née Snell), Woodbury Salterton, Devon

Sally & Ramsay Elliott, Woodbury Salterton, Devon

Audrey & David Elphick, Exton, Devon

Michael, Anna (née Summerfield), Lucy & Jenny Eyres, Woodbury, Devon

Doreen Fitzsimons, Croydon, Australia

R. Alan Foster, Ebford, Exeter, Devon

Robert Fox, Woodbury, Devon

Victor Fox, Exminster, Devon

Jennifer E. Frost, Alphington, Exeter, Devon

Mr David Fulls, Exmouth, Devon

Henry & Jennifer Fulls (née Crook), Woodbury, Devon

Austen Richard Furber, Braunston, Daventry, Northants

Bob Gaiger, Woodbury Salterton, Devon

Graham S. Gerdes, Woodbury Salterton, Devon

Bryony Giles, Woodbury, Devon

John Henry Glanvill, Woodbury, Devon

Philip J. Glanvill, Woodbury, Devon

Alan Gooding, Woodbury, Devon

Geoff Gooding, Woodbury, Devon

Derek Gooding, Woodbury, Devon

Thelma Gooding, Woodbury, Devon

D. R. Grant, South Sheilds

G. G. Grant, Woodbury, Devon

James E. Griffin, Woodbury, Devon

Julie Hall, Woodbury Salterton, Devon

William G. Hall, Budleigh Salterton, Devon

Gordon Hallett, Gulliford, Lympstone, Devon

Nicola Hammick, The Priory, Woodbury, Devon

Colin & Teresa Hart, Tadley, Hants.

Mr Clifford V. Havill, Wellington, Somerset

J. A. Hayman, Woodbury, Devon

Felicia D. Heath, Wimborne Minster, Dorset

Mrs R. B. Hitchcock, Woodbury, Devon

Richard & Gladys Hoile, Dawlish, Devon

Kenneth Hollett, Woodbury Salterton, Devon

Ruth Hugh-Jones, Pyrton, Oxon

Sara V. Hurlock, Woodbury, Devon

Margaret & Jeff Hutson, Sanderstead, South Croydon, Surrey

Mike & Joyce Jeans, Woodbury, Devon

John & Helen Jepperson (née Stokes), Newton Poppleford, Devon

David Jones, Woodbury, Devon

Sandra & Graham Joyce, Woodbury, Devon

Carolyn & David Keep, Woodbury, Devon

Edward Kenwood, New Orleans, Louisiana, USA

Ronald Kenwood, Toronto, Ontario, Canada

Clifford Kenwood, Carrboro, North Carolina, USA

Richard Kenwood, Harpenden, Hertfordshire

Ward Kenwood, New Orleans, Louisiana, USA

Joyce Kenwood Gauthier, Naples, Florida, USA

John Kirkaldy & Lesley Schlaefli, Woodbury, Devon

The Kirvan Family, Woodbury, Devon

LIST OF SUBSCRIBERS

Jenny Kyle, Canada
Kenneth G. Lang, Woodbury, Devon
Mr Ivor Loman, Northleigh, Colyton, Devon
Peter Loman, Woodbury, Devon
Anthony G. Loman, Woodbury, Exeter
Clifford J Marks, Woodbury, Devon
Mr E. W. Marlow, Stoke Gifford, Bristol
Mr & Mrs D. Mason, Manchester
Herbert & Marjorie Mason, Woodbury, Devon
Mr & Mrs Ian McFadzean, Woodbury, Devon
Marian & Derrick Mead, Woodbury, Devon
Rachel & Steve Midcalf, Woodbury, Devon
Raymond M. Middleton, Higher Mallocks, Woodbury, Devon
Mr P. Middleton, Woodbury, Devon
David J. Miles, Woodbury, Devon
G. J. & P. A. Miles, Exmouth, Devon
R. W. G. Miller, Wodbury, Devon
Mrs S. Miller, Exmouth, Devon
Mrs M. A. Missen, Exmouth, Devon
Mrs Jane Moffatt, Lympstone, Exmouth, Devon
Neil & Maureen Morton, Yorkshire
Mr & Mrs P. W. Myers, Woodbury Salterton, Devon
Paul W. Newton, Woodbury, Devon
Richard E. G. Newton, Exeter, Devon
Martin & Lin Oakley, Woodbury, Devon
Mr & Mrs R. Panter, Clyst Grange, Clyst St. Mary, Devon
Miss Caroline Parker, Salisbury, Wiltshire
Nick & Jane Parkin, Springhayes, Woodbury, Devon
Henry G. Parkinson, Goring-on-Thames, Oxfordshire
Catherine J. Parkinson, Queensland, Australia
Margaret Parkinson, Woodbury, Devon
The Payne Family, Toby Lane, Woodbury Salterton, Devon
Mr P. G. Pester, Colaton Raleigh, Sidmouth, Devon
Alan, Glenis, Megan & David Pewsey, Woodbury, Devon
Mrs Katherine Pilton (née Wakley), Up-Ottery, Devon
Marion J. Pollard (née Jones), Woodbury, Devon
Alan Pond, Exmouth, Devon
Kathy Potter (née Coles), Exeter, Devon
Eileen F. Pratt, Exton, Devon
Mr & Mrs B. W. Priddis, Woodbury, Devon
Mr G. B. Priddis, Woodbury Salterton, Devon
Ruth Ellen Prouse, The Beals, Woodbury, Devon
Mr & Mrs D. Pyatt, Woodbury, Devon
Dianne Radford, Woodbury, Devon
Mr F. D. Radford, Luton, Beds.
Muriel M. G. Radford, Woodbury, Devon
Andy Reay & Jenny Griffiths, Woodbury, Devon
Mary Sage, Exmouth, Devon
M. Joan Sangwin, Woodbury, Devon

Mrs Doreen Say (née Goss), Honiton, Devon
Gill Selley, Woodbury, Devon
Clare E. Sellick, Woodbury, Devon
Mr David J. Sellick, Woodbury, Devon
Mrs V. Seymour, Woodbury, Devon
Tony Sharland, formerly of Woodbury, Devon
Mr Raymond Shepherd, Ebford, Exeter, Devon
Ann Shields, Lympstone, Exmouth, Devon
Claire Shore, Derby
Victor & Margaret Smith, Woodbury Salterton, Devon
Sheila M. Smith, Woodbury Salterton, Devon
Ngaio G. Southard, Woodbury Salterton, Devon
Mrs I. B. Spurgeon (née Hoile), Woodbury, Devon
W. J. Stamp, Woodbury, Devon
Mrs J. Stile, Paignton, Devon
Simon & Nicola Stokes, Woodbury, Devon
Graeme W. Stokes, Glasgow, Scotland
Ian Stoyle, Thorverton, Devon
Iris L. M. Street, Woodbury, Devon
Alan C. Street, Plympton, Devon
Pamela Stuart, Woodbury, Devon
Ann Stutz, Montreal, Quebec, Canada
Pat & Barbara Summerell, Poughill, Crediton, Devon
Leonard R. Sylvester, Lympstone, Devon
Betty D. Tavender, Woodbury Salterton, Devon
Mrs Barbara N. Taverner, Woodbury/Exmouth, Devon
Margaret R. Taylor, Woodbury, Devon
John & Heather Temple, Chelmsford, Essex
Ann Templer, Woodbury, Devon
Pippa Thompson, Woodbury, Devon
Esme Thomson, Woodbury, Devon
Elizabeth & Peter Trayte, Cullompton, Devon
Joan & Peter Trevelyan, Keynsham, Bristol
Samuel G. Tucker, Woodbury Salterton, Devon
Nigel Tucker, Woodbury, Devon
Mrs A. Tucker, Woodbury, Devon
Mark Underwood, Shrewsbury
Andrew Underwood, Bolton
Phyllis Underwood, Matlock
Margaret I. Vanstone, Woodbury, Devon
Chris & Sandra Wakefield, Woodbury, Devon
Mrs Marina Wakley, Woodbury, Devon
Miss Linda Wakley, Woodbury, Devon
Eric Ware, Woodbury, Devon
Julian & Sue Ware, Streatley, Berkshire
Andrew & Christine Ware, Tamerton Foliot, Plymouth, Devon
Mrs Julie Wegner (née Wakley), Sidbury, Devon
Mrs Weilding, Woodbury, Devon
Mrs P. Whitlock, Exmouth, Devon
Sylvia Wickenden, Woodbury, Devon
Margaret Wilson, Woodbury Salterton, Devon
Alan & Maureen Wright, Woodbury, Devon

TWENTIETH CENTURY WOODBURY

Also available in the Community History Series:

The Book of Bampton Caroline Seward
The Book of Cornwood and Lutton, Photographs and Reminiscences compiled by the People of the Parish
The Ellacombe Book Sydney R. Langmead
The Book of Lamerton, A Photographic History
Lanner - A Cornish Mining Parish Sharron Schwartz and Roger Parker
The Book of Manaton
The Book of Meavy
The Book of North Newton J.C. Robins and K.C. Robins
The Book of Plymtree, The Parish and Its People compiled and edited by Tony Eames
The Book of Porlock Dennis Corner
Postbridge -The Heart of Dartmoor Reg Bellamy
The Book of Stithians, The Changing Face of a Cornish Parish Stithians Parish History Group
The Book of Torbay, A Century of Celebration Frank Pearce
The Book of Trusham Alick Cameron
Widecombe-in-the-Moor Stephen Woods
Woodbury, The Twentieth Century Revisited compiled by Roger Stokes

Further information:
If you would like to order a book or find out more about having your parish featured in this series, please contact The Editor, Community History Series, Halsgrove House, Lower Moor Way, Tiverton Business Park, Tiverton, Devon, EX16 6SS, tel: 01884 243242 or visit us at http://www.halsgrove.com
If you are interested in a particular photograph in this volume, it may be possible to supply you with a copy of the image.

Thomas Peter Daley 1847-1922 was a well read man with a great interest in history. Before becoming a postman in Woodbury and later sub postmaster, he qualified as a master mason. He kept both occupations going until he retired when his son William took over the Post Office. His grandson, John Daley, who was born in 1905 and is still going strong, tells me that it was Thomas who built the stone wall from the Fountain in Globe Hill up through The Arch to the church. This is featured on the front and back covers of this book over a span of 100 years. A job well done!

160